DOUBLE EXPOSURE

THE AMERICAN FLAG

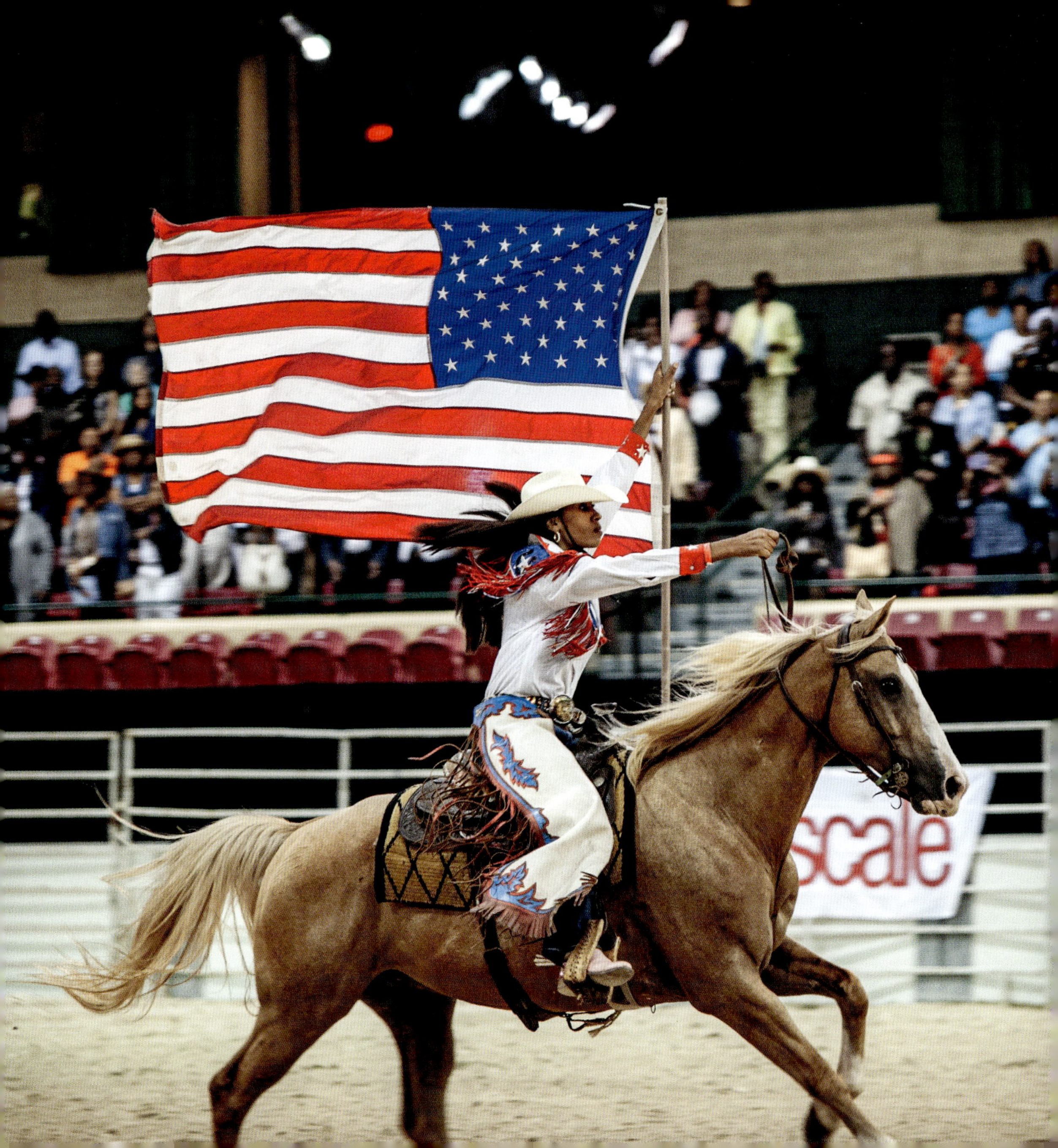

DOUBLE EXPOSURE

THE AMERICAN FLAG

Photographs from the National Museum of
African American History and Culture

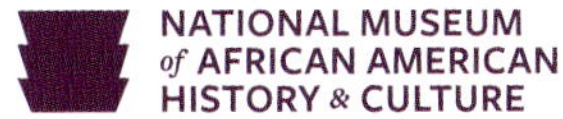

Earl W. and Amanda Stafford
Center for African American Media Arts

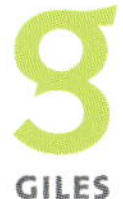

National Museum of African American History and Culture
Smithsonian Institution, Washington, D.C., in association with D Giles Limited

For the National Museum of African American History and Culture
Series Editors: Laura Coyle and Michèle Gates Moresi
Project Coordinator: Douglas Remley
Publication Committee: Aaron Bryant, Laura Coyle, Michèle Gates Moresi, Loren E. Miller, and Douglas Remley
Photograph Conservator: Mirasol Estrada

For D Giles Limited
Copyedited and proofread by Jodi Simpson
Designed by Alfonso Iacurci
Produced by GILES, an imprint of D Giles Limited
Bound and printed in Italy

Copyright © 2025 Smithsonian Institution, National Museum of African American History and Culture

First published in 2025 by GILES
An imprint of D Giles Limited
66 High Street
Lewes
BN7 1XG
gilesltd.com

EU GPSR Authorised Representative
LOGOS EUROPE, 9 rue Nicolas Poussin, 17000, LA ROCHELLE, France
E-mail: Contact@logoseurope.eu

ISBN: 978-1-913875-99-2
All measurements are in inches and centimeters; height precedes width precedes depth.

Photograph titles: Where a photographer has designated a title for his/her photograph, this title is shown in italics. All other titles are descriptive and are not italicized.

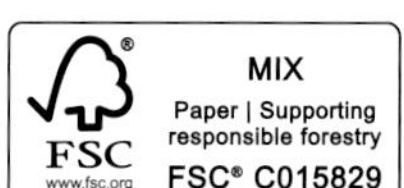

Front cover: James H. Karales, *Lewis "Big June" Marshall Carrying the U.S. Flag, Selma to Montgomery March*, March 21, 1965 (detail)
Back cover: Anthony Barboza, *Jacksonville, Fla.*, 1968
Frontispiece: Michael A. McCoy, A cowgirl carrying an American flag at a rodeo, 2014 (detail)
Page 6: Gordon Parks, *American Gothic*, 1942; printed later (detail)

FOREWORD
Laura Coyle and Michèle Gates Moresi
7

**SAY CAN YOU SEE. . .
WHAT WE SOMETIMES HAVE BEEN**
Aaron Bryant
10

PHOTOGRAPHS
17

INDEX
80

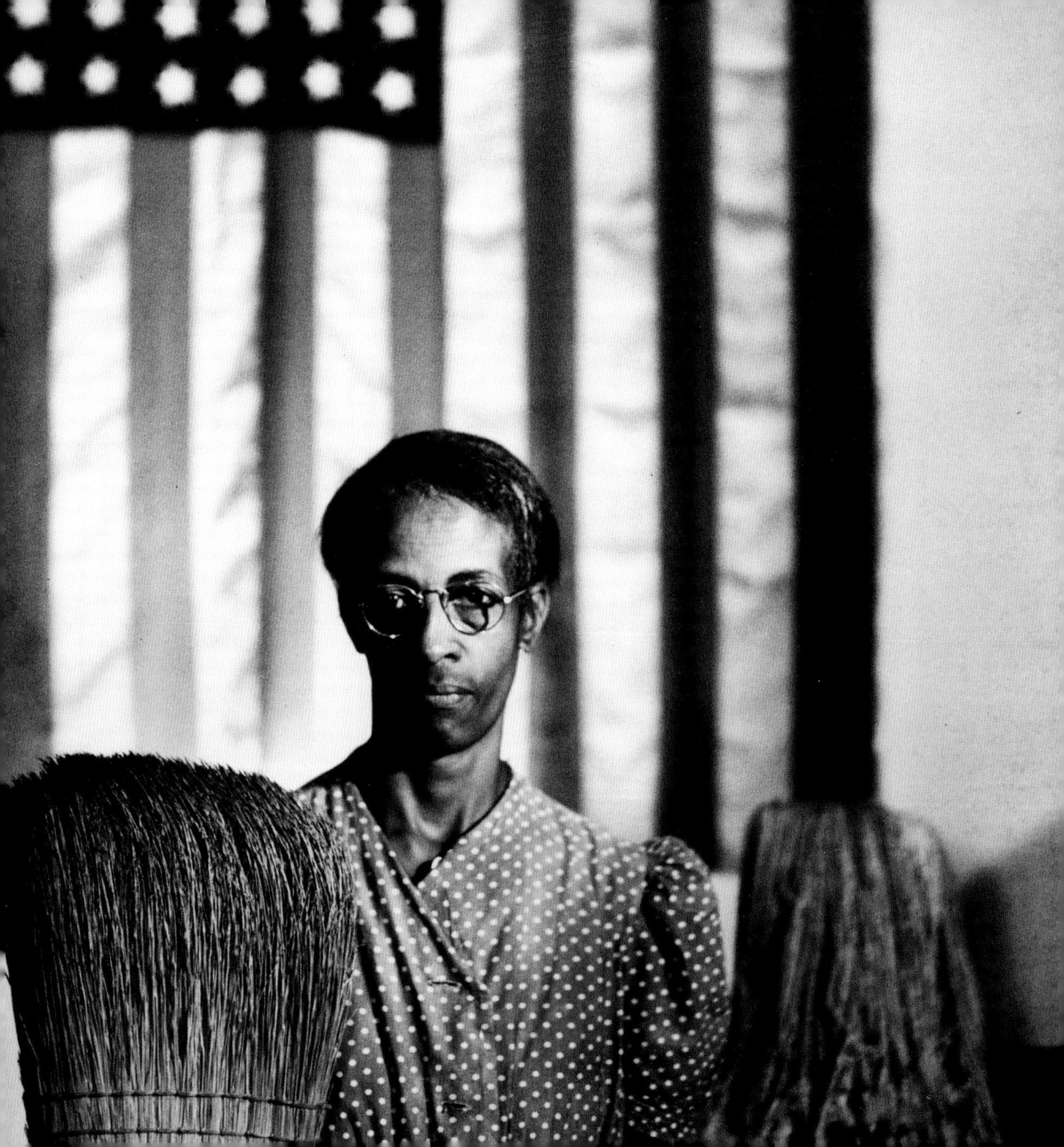

Foreword

When we asked to be the co-editors for a set of books about the photography collection at the National Museum of African American History and Culture, we had the enthusiastic support of Lonnie G. Bunch III, our Founding Director; Jacquelyn Days Serwer, the museum's first Chief Curator; and Kinshasha Holman Conwill, our former Deputy Director, along with the invaluable and capable assistance of Douglas Remley, Senior Editor / Publications Manager. But none of us imagined that we would publish ten volumes in the *Double Exposure* series, in ten years, by the tenth anniversary of the Museum.

At first, we committed to three publications: a survey of highlights from our growing collection, a volume of civil rights images, and a book of photographs of African American women. Production of these volumes coincided with the headlong race to opening, and much about those days in general and the editorial process for *Double Exposure* in particular is a blur. But what quickly came into and stayed in focus was how well these small books filled a particular need, by bringing photographs of and by African Americans to a popular audience and interpreting the images consistently from an African American perspective. We also found that no matter the topic, certain themes run through every volume: the necessity of representation, especially self-representation; the ability of photography to capture a moment; and the way photographs, as Lonnie Bunch wrote in the first foreword, have the power to move us, and "put faces and personality to historic moments."

The back cover of the first volume featured a photograph of a young woman waving an American flag (see page 9), the subject of this volume and symbol of our nation. This is fitting, because another theme that runs through these books is how complicated the experience of being an American is for so many African Americans. This volume features many different types of photographs, but in each the American flag is present, and, because it is present, it is likely to impact how the images are interpreted. The flag's presence may be purposeful or incidental, but either way, it adds complexity to the image. The United States of America is a place that means many different things to many different people. This publication coincides with celebrations surrounding the signing of the Declaration of Independence 250 years ago, a moment when revolutionaries boldly asserted that "all men are created equal," laying the foundation for the nation and democracy we continue to aspire to and enjoy. Today the United States is the envy of much of the world, but as these photographs attest, our nation is still a work in progress.

In some volumes, we arranged the photographs into sections or themes. In this publication, the photographs are presented as a continuous flow, with attention to how the photographs relate to and enrich one another. Contemporary and historic photographs, amateur snapshots alongside artistic portraits and documentary images, all present the flag with its many nuanced and complex meanings. This volume brings fresh interpretations to well-known photographs, such as Gordon Parks's *American Gothic* (see page 26) and provides a framework for interpreting less-familiar images. Take, for example, the contemporary tintype by Rashod Taylor, *The Present* (see page 37), which alludes to challenges African Americans face. In this image, the American flag as a backdrop evokes Parks's depression-era image while the hoodie brings to mind more recent events. Together we hope the images enrich understanding of the depth and variety of the African American experience. Further context is added to the topic and photos through an essay by Aaron Bryant that focuses on the American flag as a varied symbol for what it means to be an American.

This tenth volume in the series is realized thanks to many other people who have collaborated on this important book. Special acknowledgement goes to the other members of our Publication Team: Aaron Bryant, Curator of Photography, Visual Culture, and Contemporary History; Loren E. Miller, Museum Specialist; and Douglas Remley, Senior Editor / Publications Manager and Project Coordinator for the series. We'd like to extend a special thanks to Michelle Joan Wilkinson for providing her expertise and knowledge on African Americans and the American flag during the development of this project. A word of thanks also goes to Mirasol Estrada, Photographs Conservator, and the Office of Collections Management, for their work in preparing many of these photographs for inclusion in the book, while ongoing support and encouragement from the Museum's senior leadership, including Deputy Director Michelle D. Commander, has been invaluable to the continuation of the series.

We are also very fortunate to have the pleasure of co-publishing with D Giles Limited. At Giles, the team would like particularly to thank Dan Giles, Managing Director; Alfonso Iacurci, Designer; Allison McCormick, Managing Editor; Louise Ramsay, Production Manager; Jodi Simpson, copyeditor and proofreader; and Liz Japes, Sales and Marketing Manager. Finally, we would like to thank our Museum's Digitization Team for researching, cataloguing, and digitizing the images included in this volume.

With this volume, we are stepping down from our roles as co-editors, one of the most fulfilling experiences in our careers. Our role was to foster a collaborative process, to come up with coherent selections of photographs, and to assist authors in shaping their essays with the goal of enriching readers' experience of images. The greatest pleasures we had working on these volumes were the joy of looking at these photographs together, the delight in making unexpected connections, and, in the process of winnowing down our selection from a collection that now numbers more than 19,000, the gratification of learning so much we did not know about each topic and the photographs. We hope that our readers, as they peruse this volume of photographs of African Americans with the American flag and earlier volumes in the series, enjoy a similar sense of satisfaction.

Laura Coyle and Michèle Gates Moresi
Co-editors, Double Exposure Series

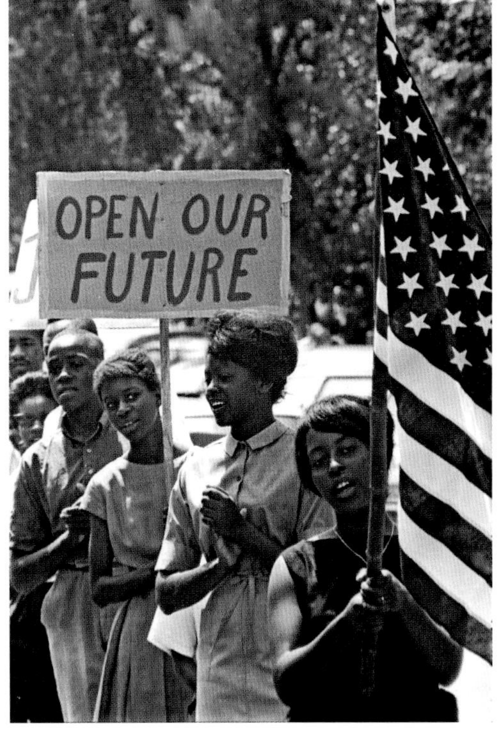

***July 4 March Through
Chapel Hill***, 1964
James H. Wallace Jr.

Say Can You See…
What We Sometimes Have Been

Aaron Bryant
National Museum of African American History and Culture

n Maurice Sorrell's poignant image of renowned civil rights activists Fannie Lou Hamer and Ella Baker, an exhausted but defiant Hamer holds the American flag slightly below her heart, not only to affirm her Americanism but to demand its recognition. A former sharecropper in the cotton fields of the Mississippi Delta, Hamer worked with Baker and the Student Nonviolent Coordinating Committee (SNCC) to organize the 1964 Freedom Summer campaign, also known as the Mississippi Summer Project. Activists from across the country traveled to Mississippi to mobilize and register African American voters. They protested the state's discriminatory and often violent practices of denying and suppressing Black voters and their votes. Earlier that year, Hamer, Baker, and a host of other organizers formed the Mississippi Freedom Democratic Party (MFDP) to challenge Mississippi's whites-only political process. On August 6, the MFDP held its state convention at the Masonic Temple in Jackson, where Sorrell captured this moment while covering the event for the Johnson Publishing Company. The first African American admitted to the White House News Photographers Association, Sorrell documented a critical shift in American politics through photography.

This book features powerful photographs such as Sorrell's that show the American flag in meaningful moments of American history. The nation's most recognizable emblem, the flag is a symbol of democratic ideals as well as its realities. Here, it serves as a defiant symbol in the fight for voting rights in Mississippi. It is also used as a weapon, as seen in an iconic photograph by Stanley Forman, who captures an attack over arguments about school desegregation in Boston (see page 13). The flag can also reflect the nation's proudest moments, as in a photograph of U.S. Olympians celebrating victory (see page 15). Each photographer in this collection captures what the flag means to the American people.

In reflecting on images of the United States flag, what do you see? What values and events come to mind? For many people, the flag represents the American dream and the

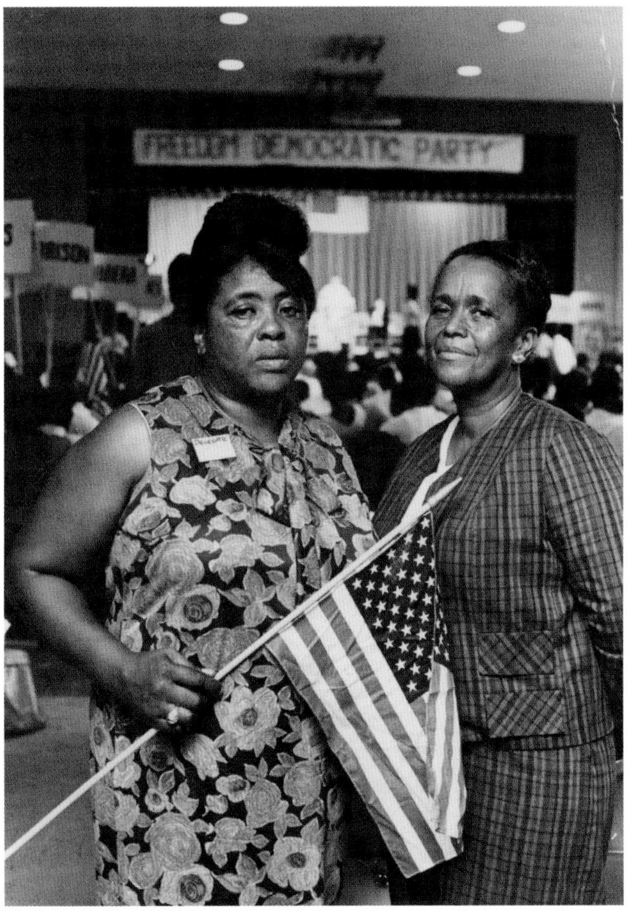

Fannie Lou Hamer and Ella Baker at the Mississippi Freedom Democratic Party Convention, Jackson, Mississippi, August 1964
Maurice Sorrell

promise of equality, freedom, and opportunity. It communicates the ideals of a democracy that guarantees fairness in the shaping of laws that affect our lives and the nation's future. The flag symbolizes justice and the rights and burdens of citizenship, while representing the ideas and histories that have been the nation's greatest strength and its most enduring challenge. While some Americans saw liberty in dawn's early light, others sought freedom in a dusk lit by the light of northern stars. As photographs in this publication suggest, the significance of an image and symbol transcends what we can see. The flag's meaning is as varied as the people who make up this nation.

The photograph of Hamer and Baker was featured on the cover of Johnson Publishing Company's August 27, 1964, issue of *Jet* magazine with the cover line "Mississippi Freedom Party May Change Dixie Vote Pattern." Just days before, Hamer had delivered a powerful testimony at the Democratic National Committee convention in Atlantic City, New Jersey, where the MFDP had elected sixty-eight delegates to represent them. Hamer challenged the political representation of Mississippi's all-white delegation, emphatically ending her testimony with a pointed question to the credentials committee and all Americans:

"Is this America, the land of the free and the home of the brave, where we have to sleep with our telephones off of the hooks because our lives be threatened daily, because we want to live as decent human beings, in America?"[1] Despite Hamer's compelling appeal for the formal recognition and seating of the MFDP delegates as part of the national convention, the credentials committee refused.

Fearing Hamer's speech would alienate white voters in the South, President Lyndon Johnson quickly called a news conference to interrupt national coverage of her testimony. A portion of Hamer's testimony was broadcast nationwide, however, which drew national attention to the violence and injustice of voter suppression. One year after Sorrell captured the moment through this image, President Johnson signed the Voting Rights Act into law on August 6, 1965. Despite losing the support of Southern segregationists in the Democratic Party, often called Dixicrats, who left to join the Republican Party, Hamer's speech inspired the nationwide protests that gained crucial public support to convince Johnson to sign the legislation.

While the flag in Sorrell's image of Hamer and Baker symbolizes demands for full participation and citizenship, *The Soiling of Old Glory*, by Pulitzer Prize–winning photographer Stanley Forman demonstrates

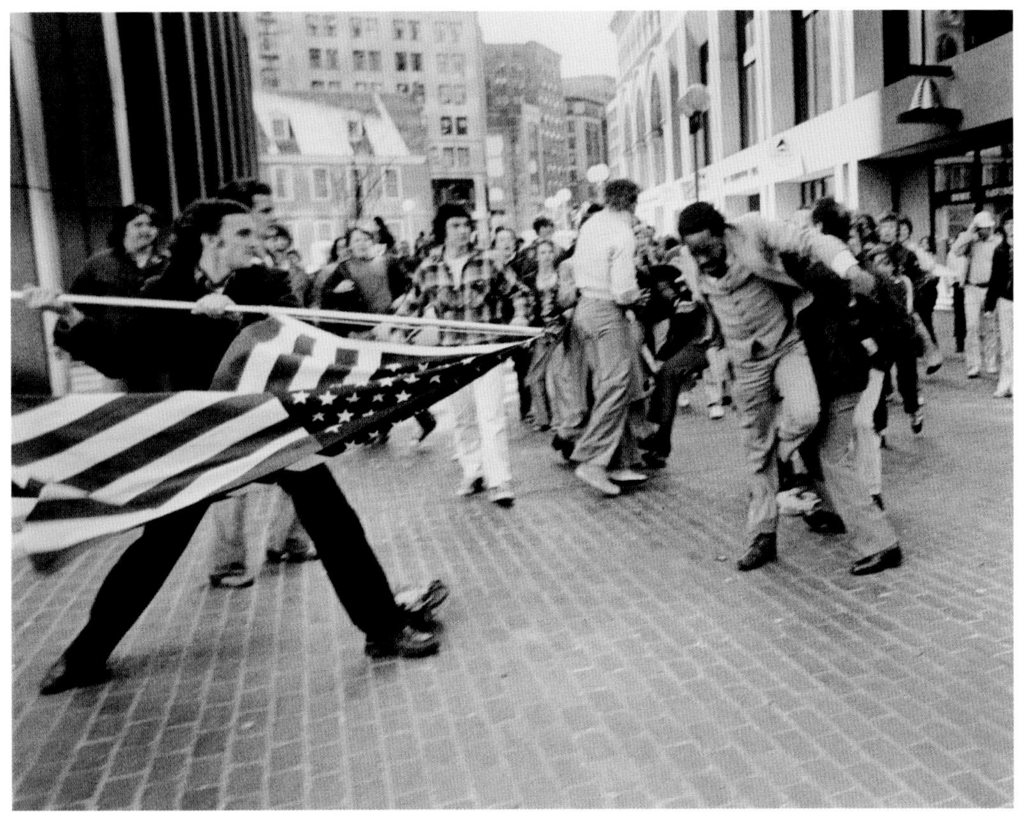

The Soiling of Old Glory,
April 5, 1976
Stanley Forman

that the American flag has sometimes been used as a weapon of tyranny and exclusion. Forman captured this image in 1976, when school desegregation and busing in Boston were violently contentious issues. In 1974, a federal court required the city to address segregation in public education by busing African American students to predominantly white schools and white students to schools in Black communities. By 1976, anti-busing protests had escalated into a crisis of riots and physical confrontations.

Forman photographed Joseph Rakes, a white teenager, using the American flag to attack Theodore (Ted) Landsmark, an African American lawyer and activist. Landsmark was walking to a meeting in Boston's City Hall when he was assaulted by anti-busing protesters, and, in seconds, Forman captured a series of images that documented the confrontation. Landsmark was knocked to the ground and suffered several injuries, including a broken nose, and although Rakes was convicted of assault with a deadly weapon, his two-year sentence was suspended, and he was put on probation.

As tensions in Boston erupted, national interest turned to the racial and economic divides in cities across the country. Charles Glenn, director of urban education and equity for the Massachusetts Department

of Education, was responsible for the administration of state funds for magnet schools and school desegregation. As he recalled, "In the middle of all this chaos, I wrote in my journal, *Fiat justitia ruat caelum*: Do justice, though the heavens fall. I remember reflecting then, 'What good will it do to do justice if the heavens fall and what would justice look like among the ruins?'"[2] Many of the subjects in these photographs, like Hamer and Baker, however, would challenge Glenn to consider the generations that have lived in the ruins of injustice. As W. E. B. Du Bois once wrote, "the cost of liberty is less than the price of repression."[3] Today, Landsmark is a distinguished professor of public policy and urban affairs at Northeastern University and director of the Kitty and Michael Dukakis Center for Urban and Regional Policy, where he no doubt draws from his experiences decades ago to encourage new generations of students to reflect on the price of justice and what it means to be an American.

Eight years after Forman photographed Landsmark in Boston, Carl Lewis made history during the 1984 Summer Olympic Games in Los Angeles, California. That year, Lewis won four gold medals in track and field, which made him the first American to accomplish such a feat since Jesse Owens in 1936. Taken after the medal ceremonies and U.S. victory

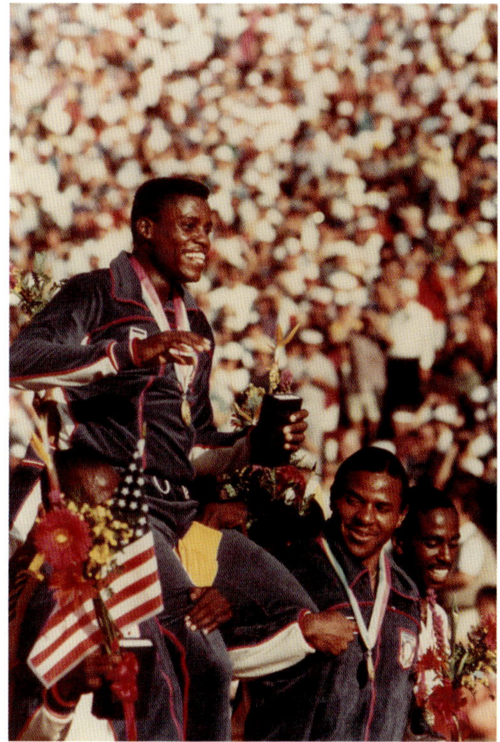

Carl Lewis after winning his fourth gold medal at the Los Angeles Olympics, 1984
Unidentified photographer

in the 4 x 100 meters relay, the photograph celebrates Lewis and his teammates' achievements. At first glance, we see a team of Olympians celebrating, with Lewis on their shoulders, holding gold medals against the backdrop of the American flag and a stadium packed with spectators. But the photograph also communicates a history that reaches beyond the image itself.

In 1984, as America displayed and broadcast its pride on the Olympic stage, the games marked a difficult period in global politics. That year, fourteen Eastern Bloc countries, including the Soviet Union and East Germany, boycotted the Olympics in response to the American boycott of the 1980 Summer Olympics in Moscow. The 1980 boycott protested the Soviet invasion of Afghanistan in 1979, which marked a pivotal moment in the Cold War. Soviet forces occupied Afghanistan for nearly a decade and the costs associated with the occupation are considered a contributing factor to the eventual decline of communism and the fall of the Soviet Union. In 1984, as Soviet and communist influence around the world weakened, the United States dominated the Olympics and America rose as a global model of freedom and exceptionalism.

The photograph of Lewis and his teammates reflects these ideas through the unity of their uniforms, their success as a relay team, and the American flag they carry to celebrate their Olympic win. Additionally, the team, which included Sam Graddy, Ron Brown, Calvin Smith, and Lewis, broke a world record, winning Lewis his fourth gold medal at the summer games. While the Olympics were held at a time in which the Soviet Union threatened to spread communism in the Middle East, four African Americans represented democracy on a global stage, setting new standards in track and field. Lewis sits on his teammates' shoulders, and at the bottom left we see Graddy carrying both Lewis and the American flag. Here, the photographer presents the team as compatriots who celebrate the best in American values.

These and other images in this publication represent a history of American values, dreams, and realities. As Ted Landsmark once reflected, in remembering his experiences in Boston, "I view myself as an American who has benefited tremendously from the best America can provide. And I also recognize that in the name of the flag some very heinous things have been done to people in this country and elsewhere." Landsmark continued, "When there's a demonstration that involves the flag, that speaks to how we express our values of democracy and fairness . . . it is really an appropriate icon for all of us to look to as to what we want to be, as

opposed to what we sometimes have been."[4] This collection of photographs encourages a similar reflection—as 2026 marks the 250th anniversary of the nation's founding, now is the time to reflect on a past where we sometimes lived up to our ideals and sometimes fell far short, and to envision a shared future of what we want to be.

Endnotes

1. Fannie Lou Hamer, testimony before the Credentials Committee, Democratic National Convention, August 22, 1964, American Rhetoric Online Speech Bank, last updated August 19, 2022, https://www.americanrhetoric.com/speeches/fannielouhamercredentialscommittee.htm.
2. PBS, *The Busing Battleground: The Decades-Long Road to School Desegregation*, American Experience, October 3, 2023, video, 1:52:30, https://www.pbs.org/wgbh/americanexperience/films/busing-battleground/.
3. W. E. B. Du Bois, *John Brown* (Philadelphia: George W. Jacobs & Company, 1909), available online at Project Gutenberg, https://www.gutenberg.org/cache/epub/62799/pg62799-images.html.
4. Bill Chappell, "Life after Iconic Photo: Today's Parallels of American Flag's Role in Racial Protest," NPR, September 18, 2016, https://www.npr.org/2016/09/18/494442131/life-after-iconic-photo-todays-parallels-of-american-flags-role-in-racial-protes.

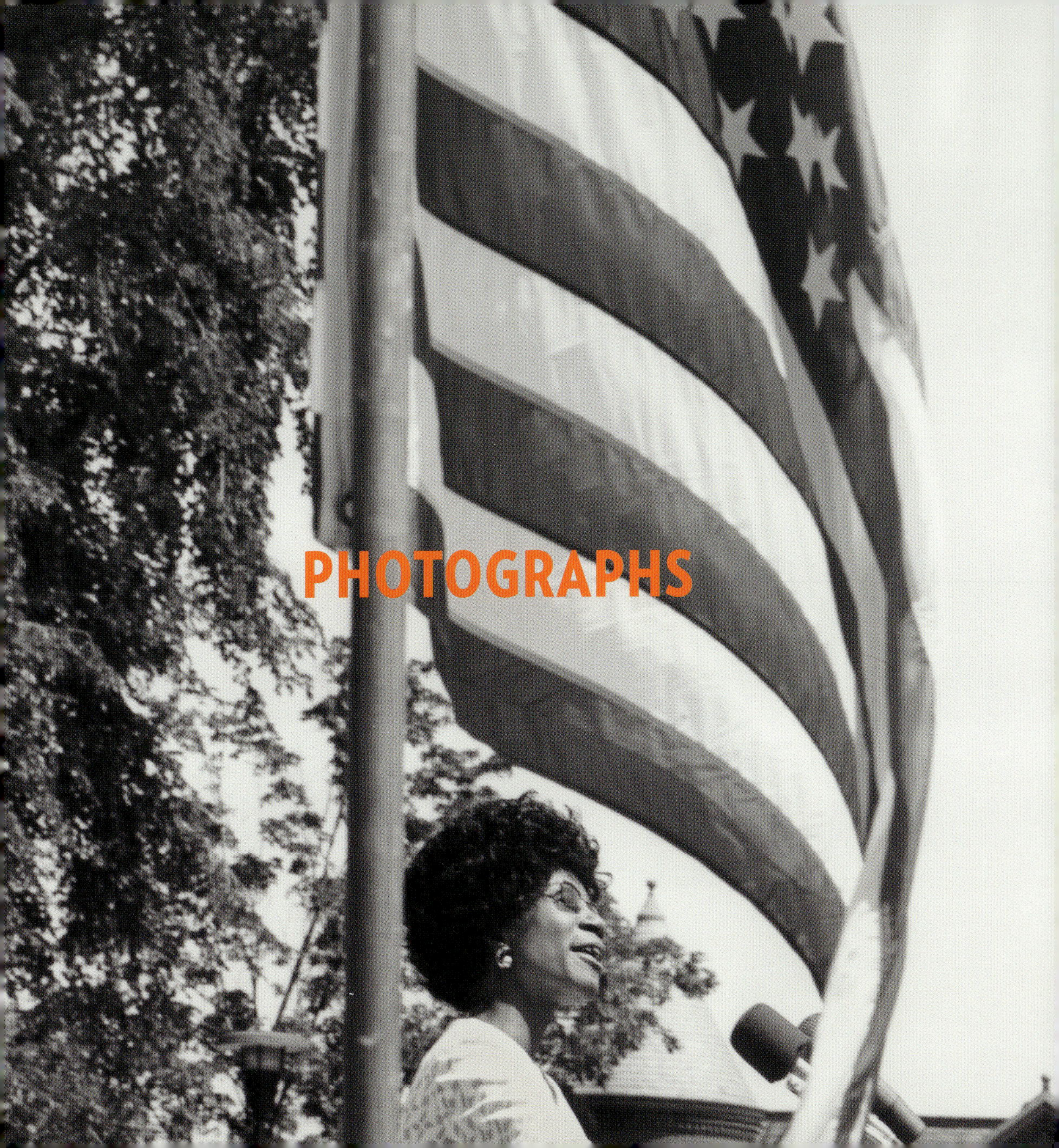
PHOTOGRAPHS

**A cowgirl carrying
an American flag at a
rodeo**, 2014
Michael A. McCoy

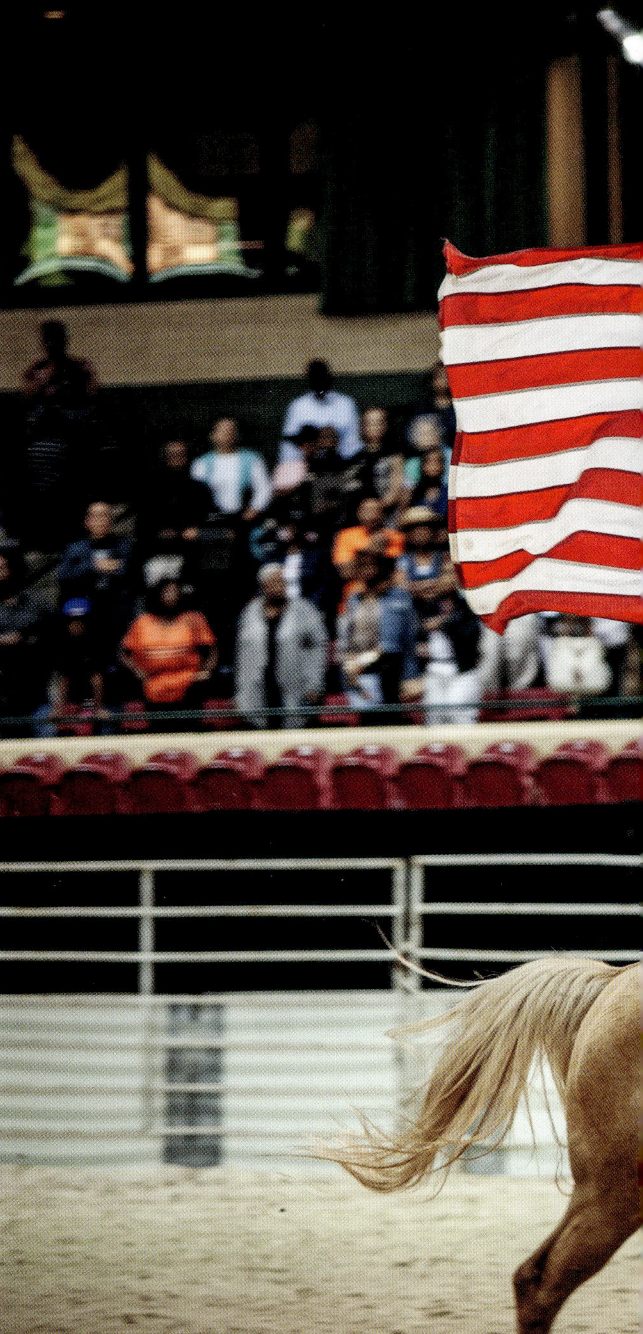

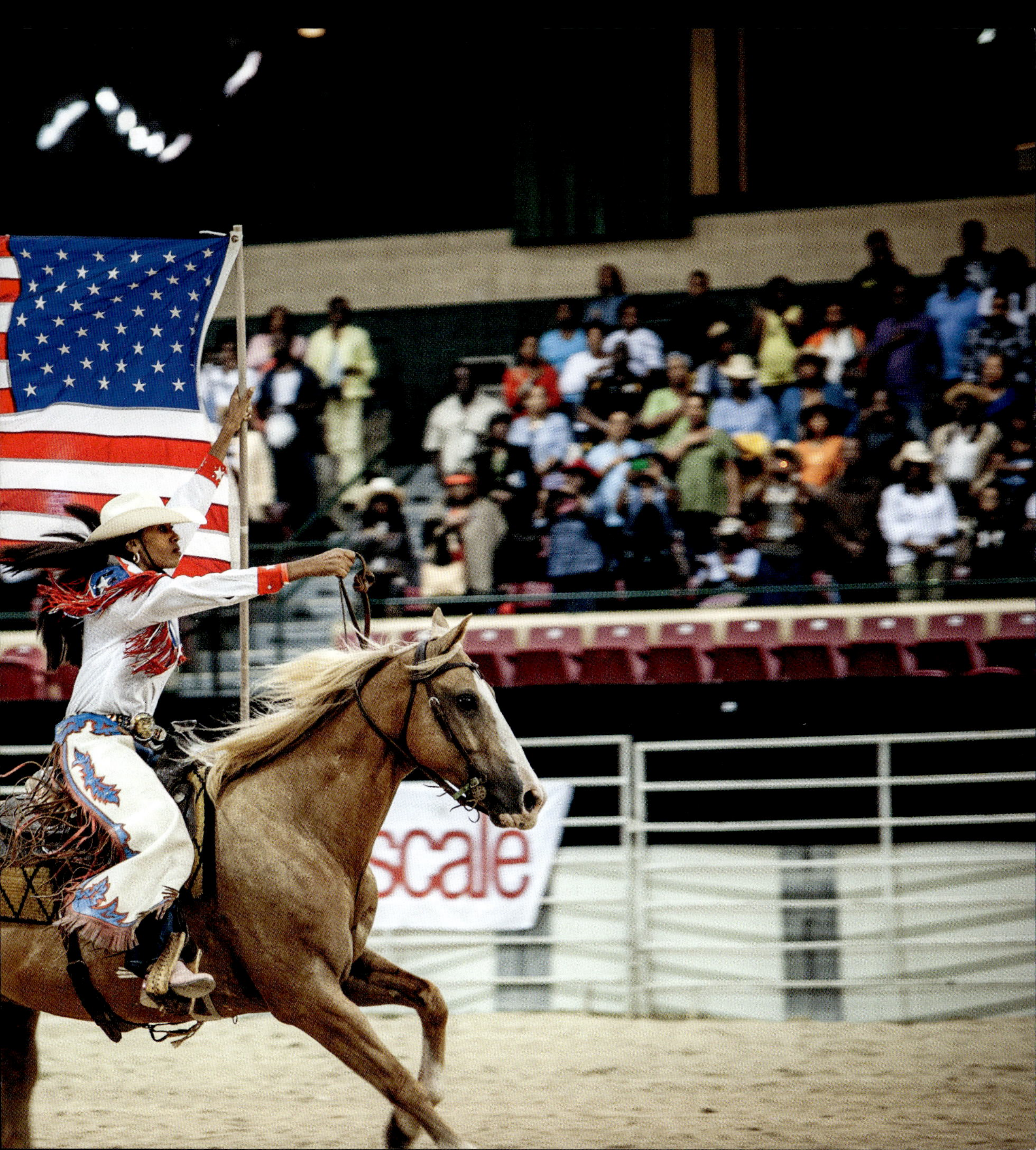

Congresswoman Shirley Chisholm speaks at the Mary McLeod Bethune Statue Commemoration Celebration, Lincoln Park, Washington, D.C., 1971
Maurice Sorrell

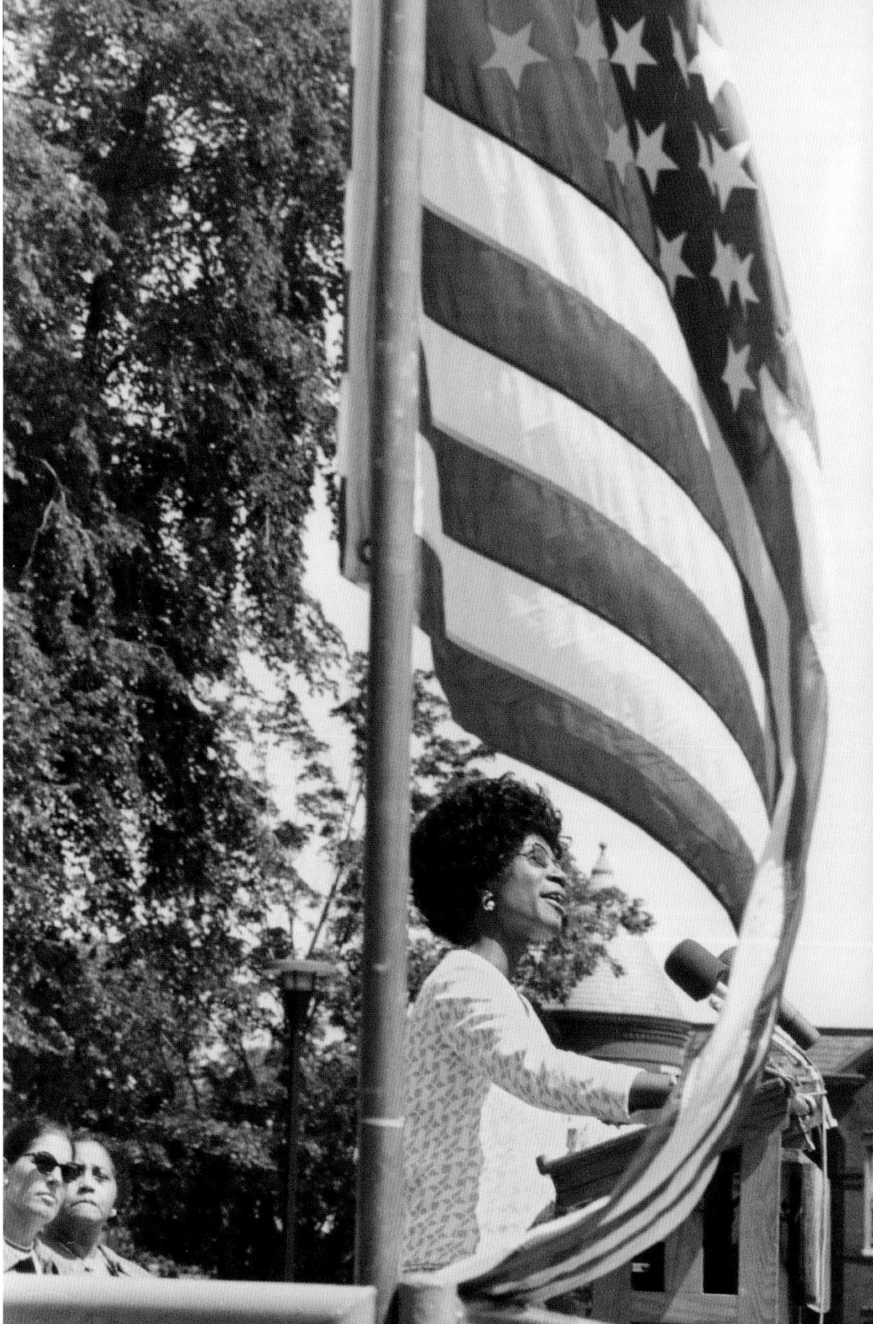

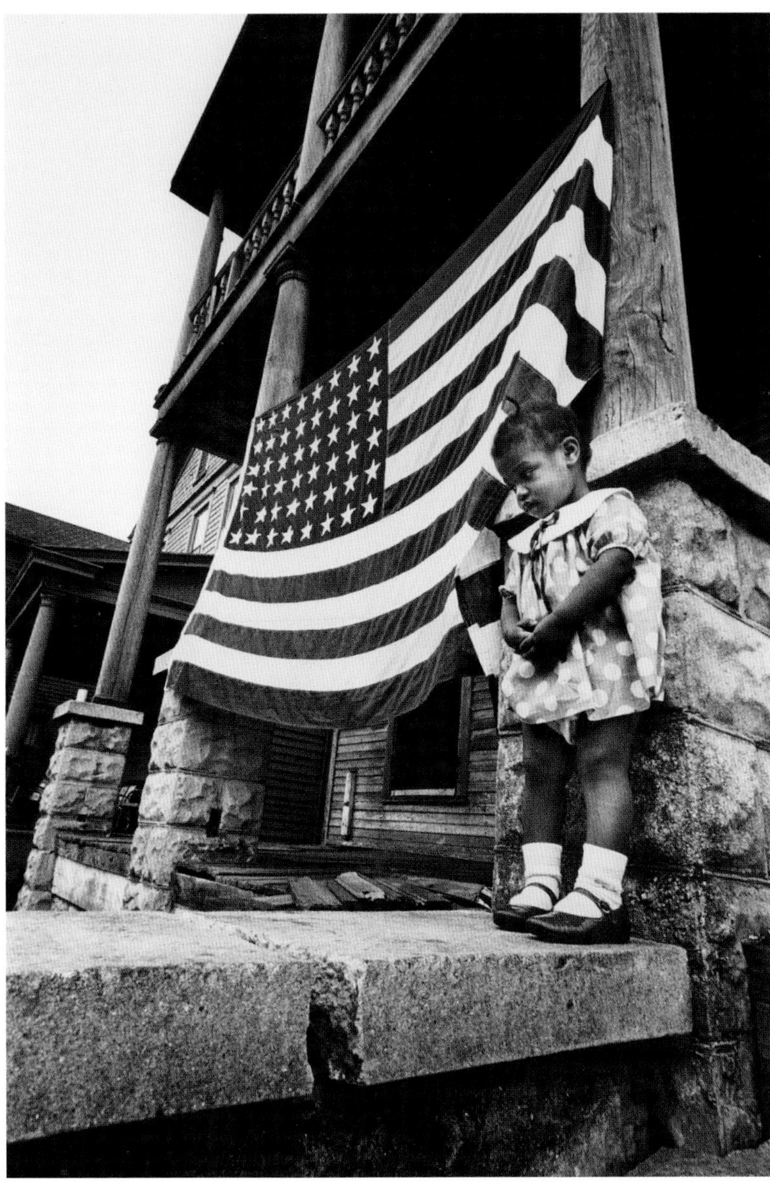

Jacksonville, Fla.,
1968
Anthony Barboza

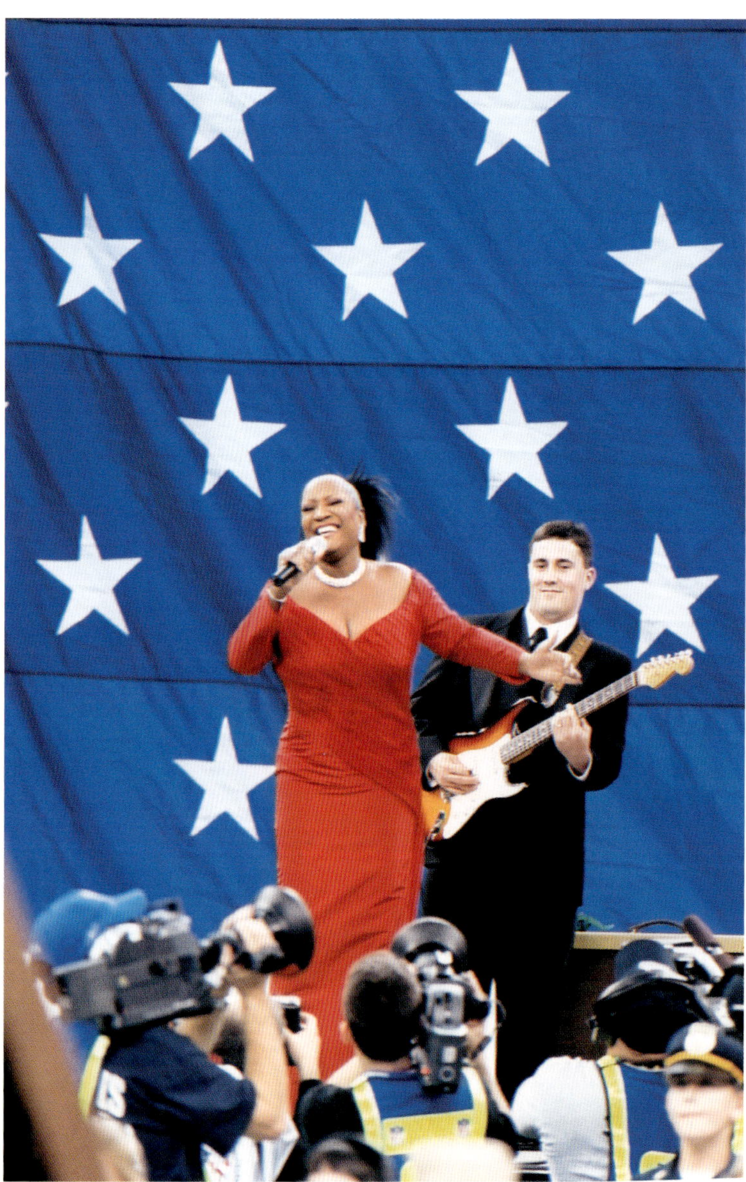

Patti LaBelle performing during the pregame show of Super Bowl XXXVI, February 3, 2002
Vandell Cobb

—

During the Super Bowl XXXVI pregame show in New Orleans, Louisiana, Patti LaBelle joined Yolanda Adams, James Ingram, Wynonna Judd, and Barry Manilow in a performance of the song "Let Freedom Ring" in a tribute to those killed in the September 11, 2001, terrorist attacks.

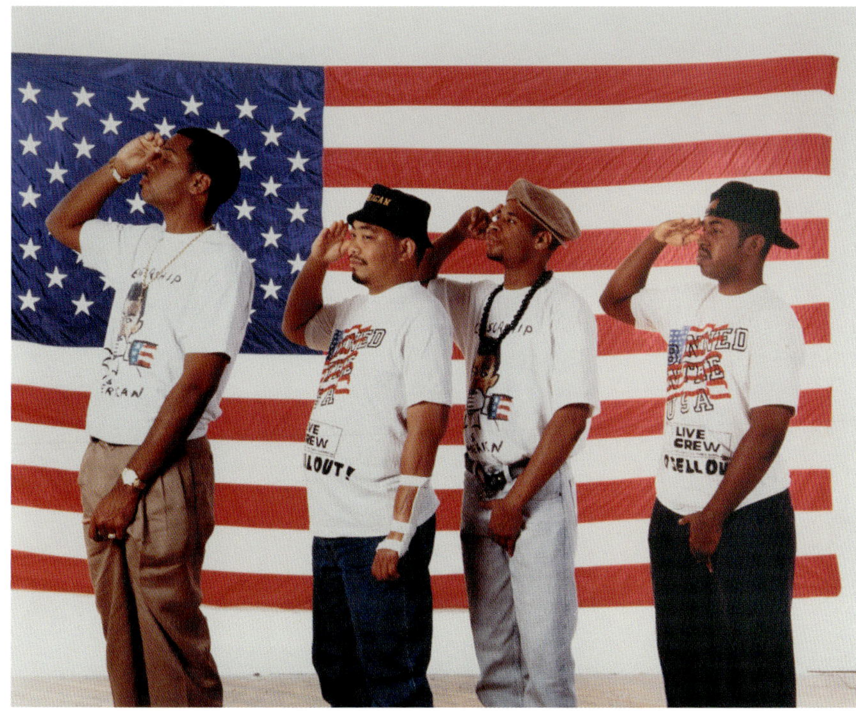

Luther Campbell and the 2 Live Crew, 1990
Janette Beckman

Carl Lewis after winning his fourth gold medal at the Los Angeles Olympics, 1984
Unidentified photographer

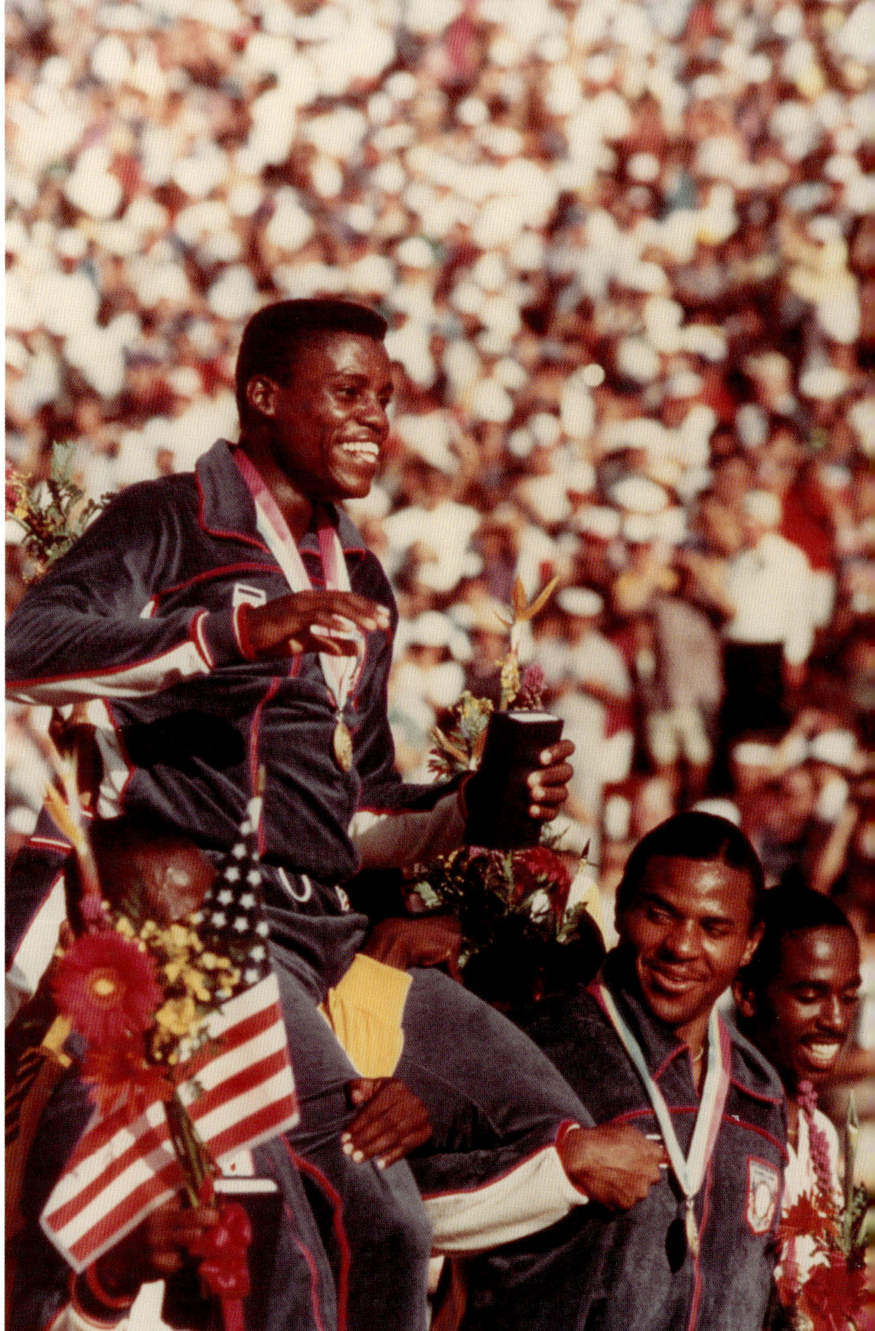

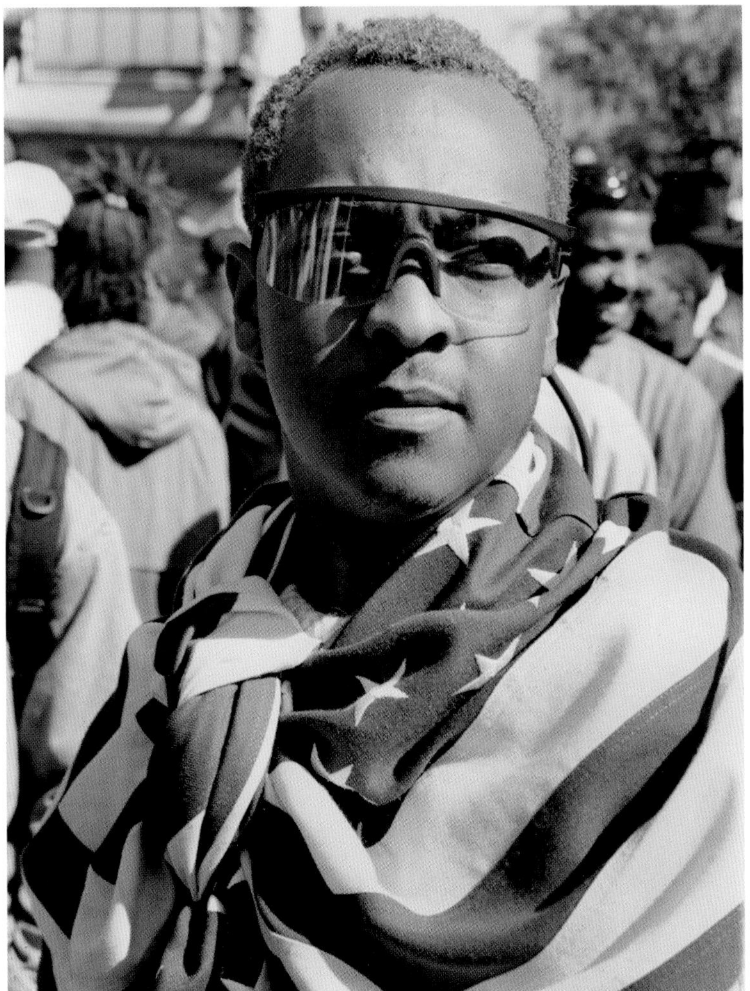

Flag Around Neck,
October 16, 1995
From the series ***One Million Strong***
Roderick Terry
—
An attendee at the Million Man March in Washington, D.C.

American Gothic,
1942; printed later
Gordon Parks
—
Legendary photographer
Gordon Parks used his
camera as a weapon to
fight injustice. In one of
his most iconic images,
Ella Watson, a woman who
cleaned the government
building where Parks
worked, solemnly holds
a broom and mop in front
of the American flag.
Parks spent a month
photographing Watson
and learning about her
life. She struggled to
support her family and
could not get a better
job, despite having the
same education and
credentials as white
women performing office
work. Parks's photograph
highlights the injustices
Watson faced as a Black
woman in America.

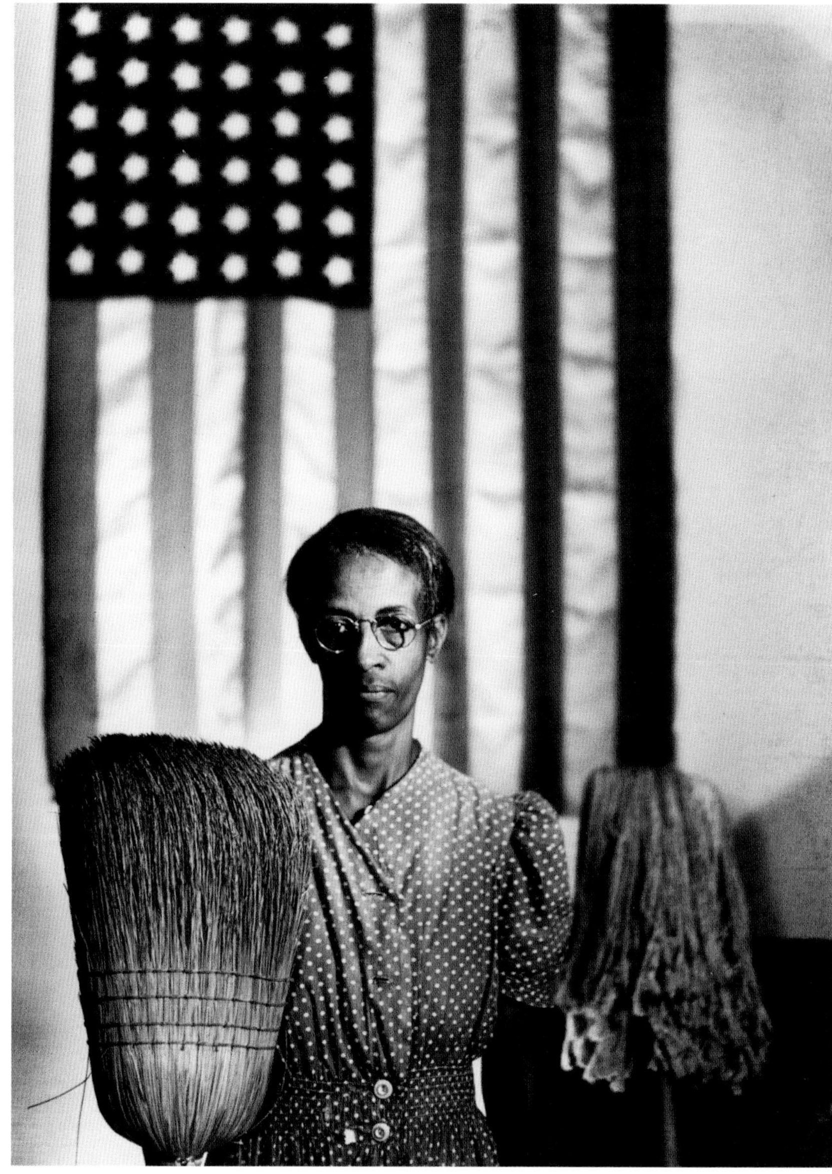

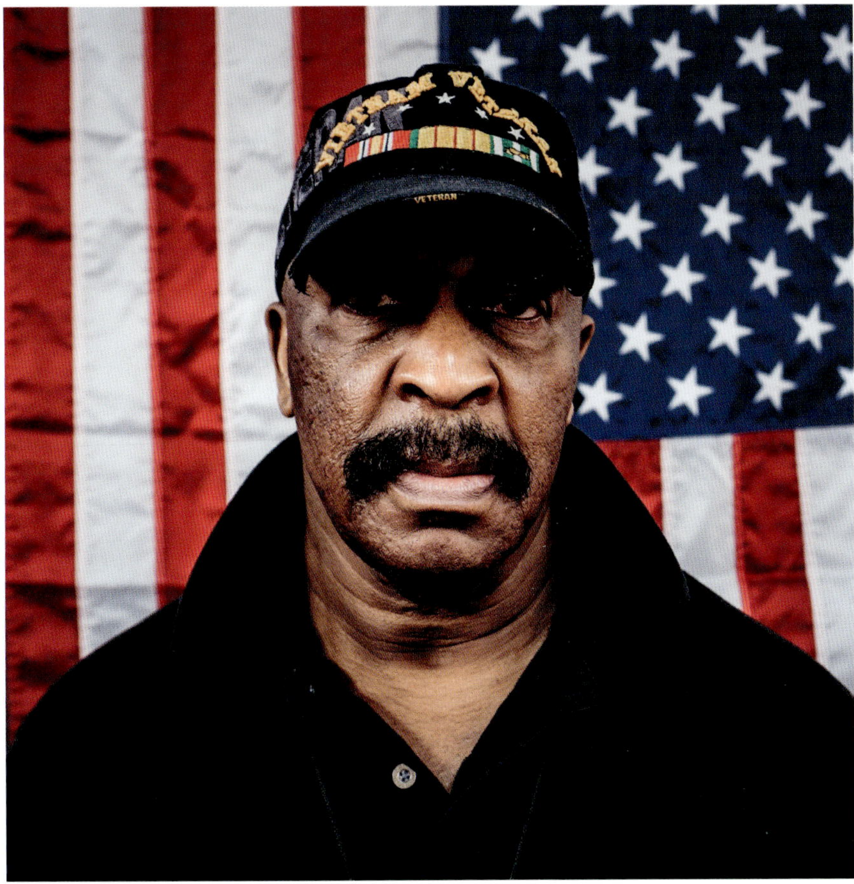

Vietnam veteran, Martinsburg, West Virginia, 2017
Michael A. McCoy

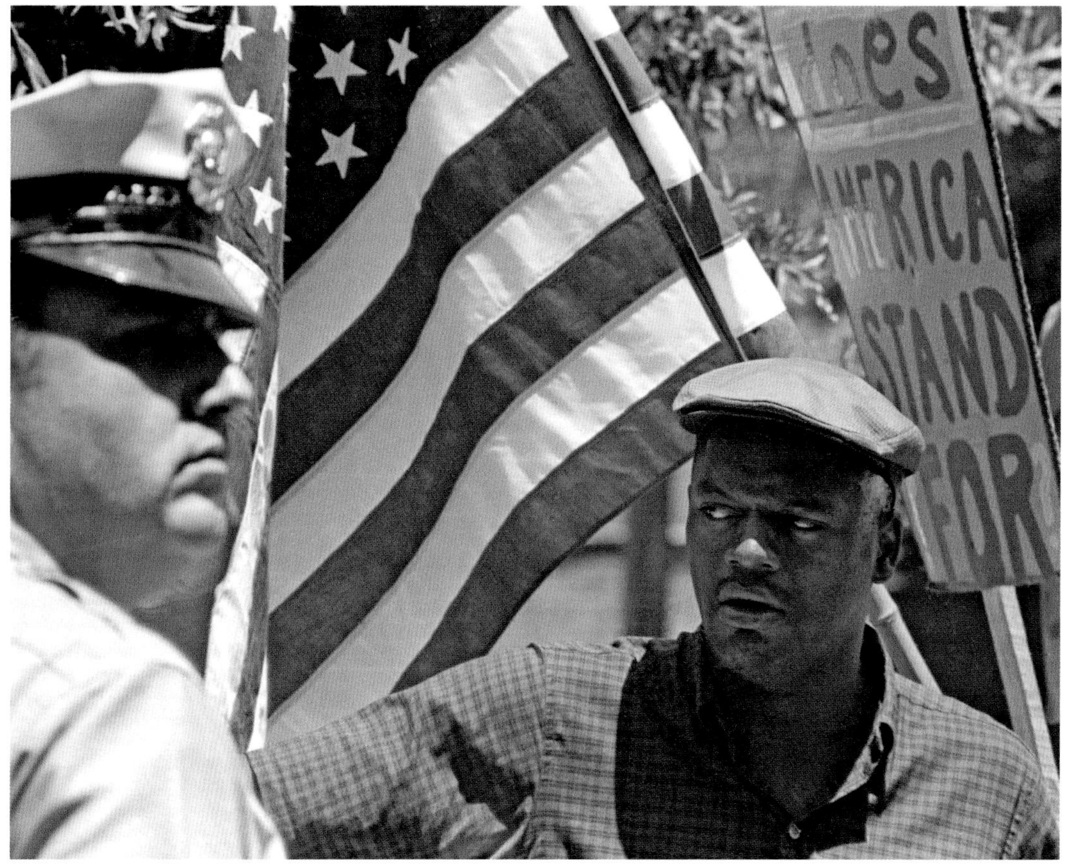

Activist Leader Hillard Caldwell with American Flag, Facing a Policeman During a Demonstration, 1964
James H. Wallace Jr.

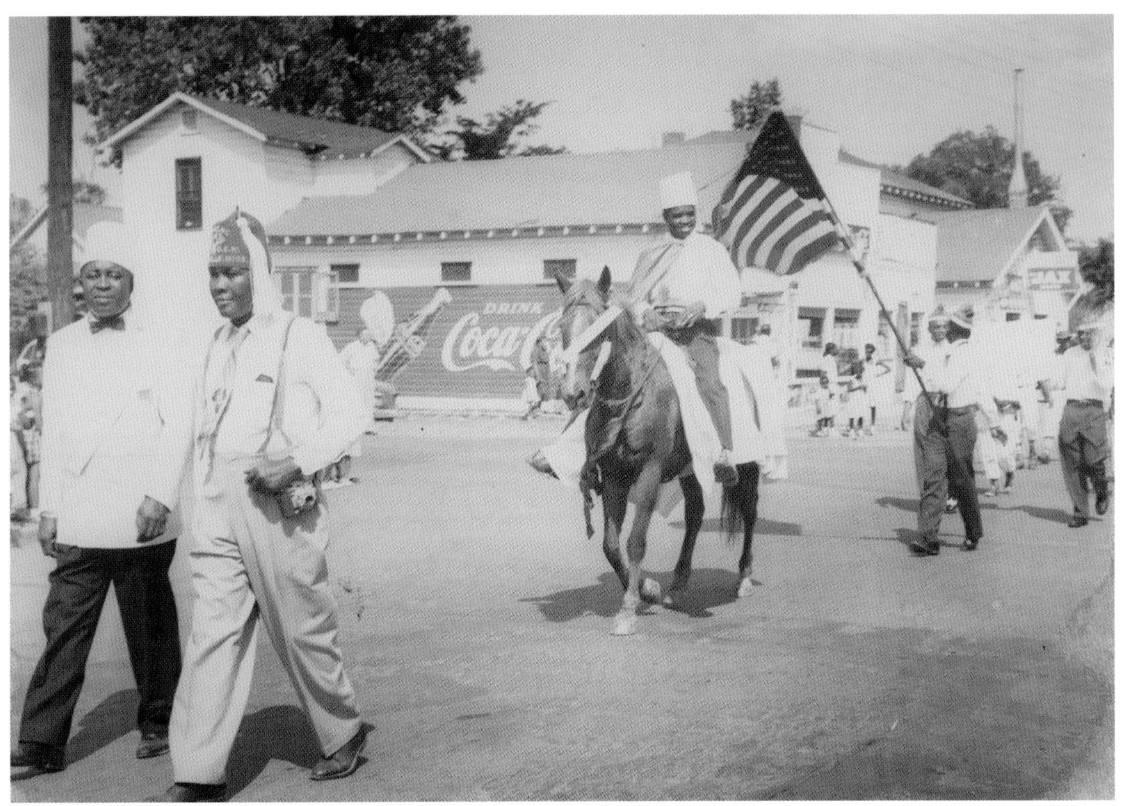

**Members of the Improved Benevolent
Protective Order of Elks of the World
during a parade in Greenville, Mississippi,**
mid-20th century
Rev. Henry Clay Anderson

Helen Jackson, Supreme Court seamstress, 1957
Gaston DeVigne

—

This photograph of Helen Jackson was taken for a May 1957 feature in *Ebony* magazine. In addition to mending the robes worn by the Justices, Jackson also repaired flags and building employees' uniforms, and made draperies for use in the building.

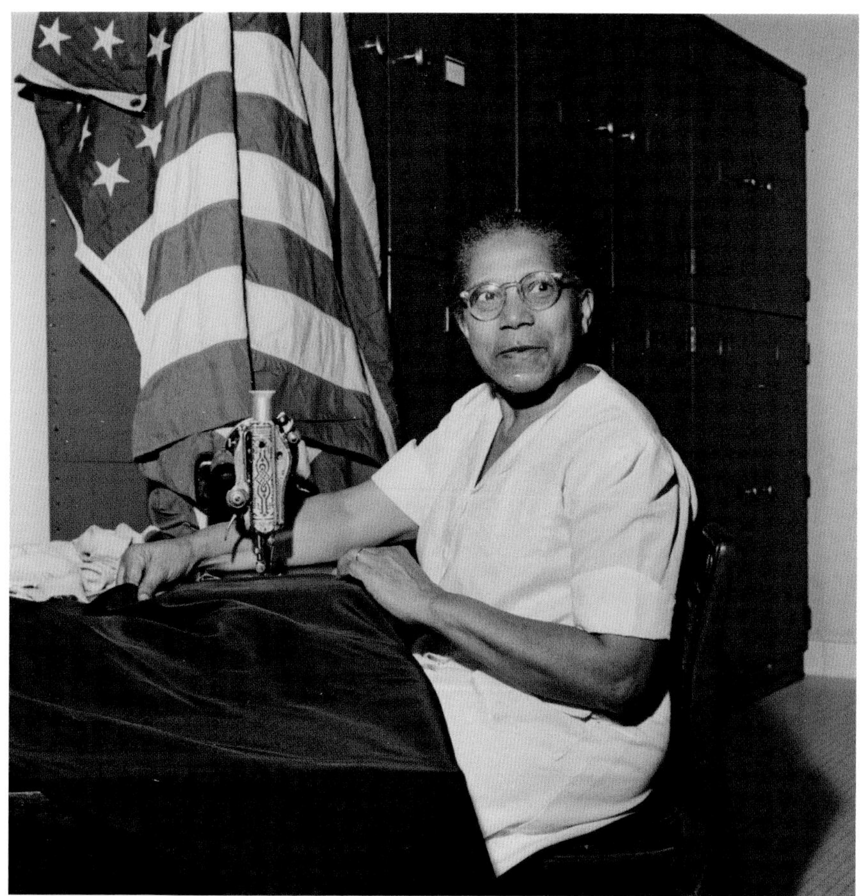

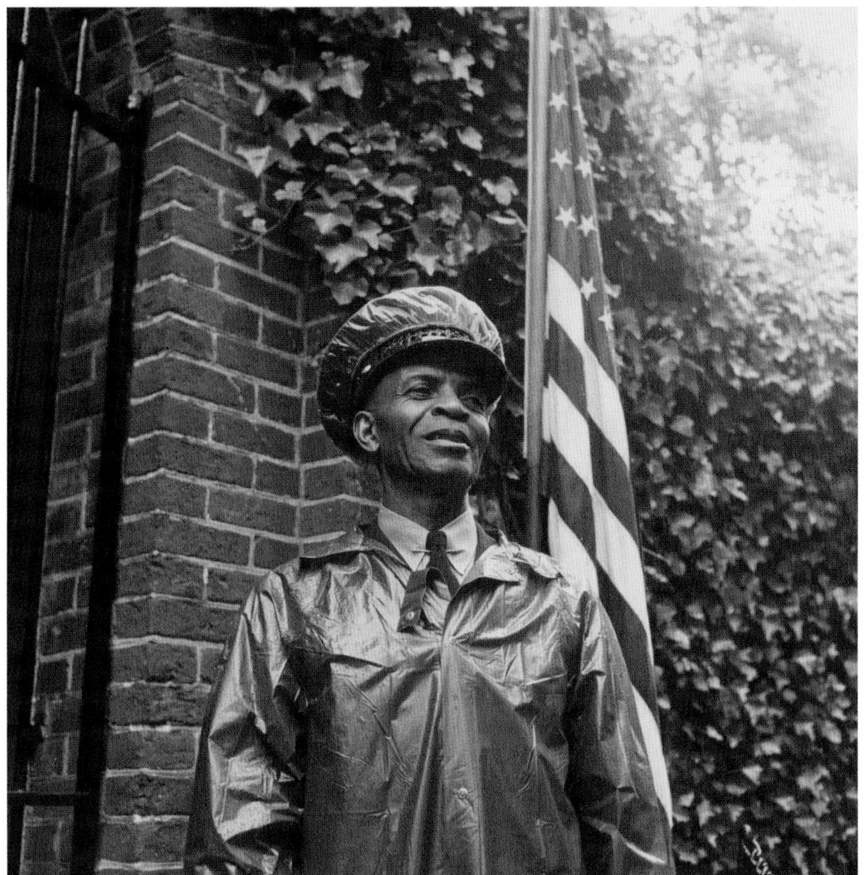

Will Holland guarding George Washington's tomb, 1955
Bertrand Miles
—
For more than sixty years, Will Holland worked at Mount Vernon, serving thirty years as the head guard outside the vault housing George and Martha Washington's tombs. Holland, who succeeded his father-in-law, George Ford, as tomb-watcher in 1935, served as both a watchman and a lecturer, ensuring decorum in this sacred space while informing visitors of the history of Washington's burial place.

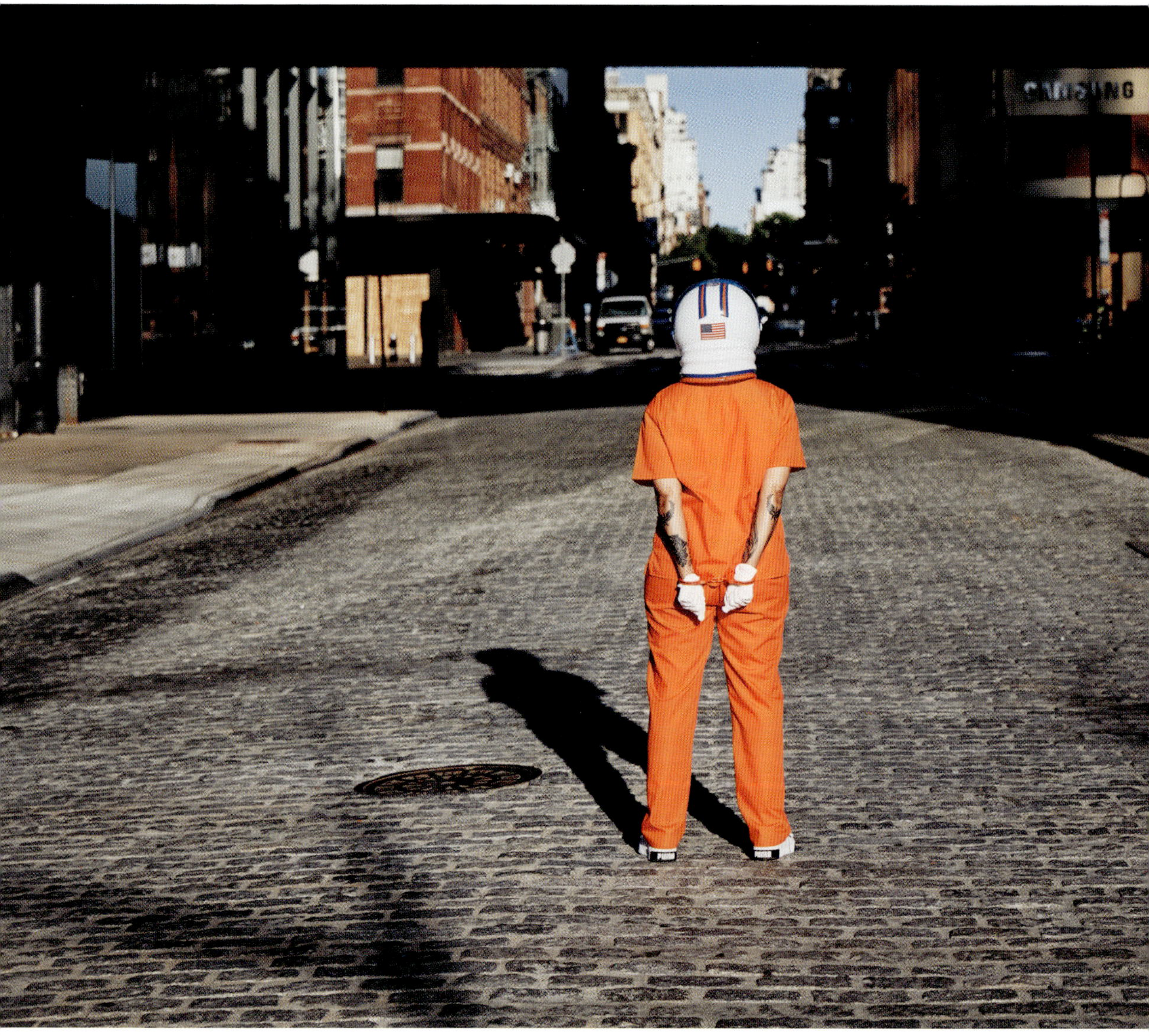

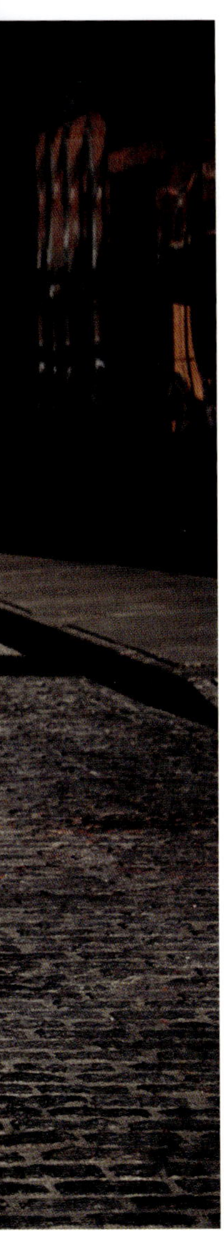

Back at You, 2020
From the series
syzygy, the vision
Lola Flash

—

Standing in isolation
during the COVID-19
pandemic, photographer
and activist Lola Flash
wears a space helmet
and a prison uniform
while their hands are
handcuffed behind their
back. The photograph
is part of Flash's self-
portrait series *syzygy, the
vision*, which explores the
institutionalized systems
that bind us to our past,
present, and future.
With the American flag
sticker on their helmet,
Flash depicts a proud
American astronaut who
is nonetheless treated
as a criminal and taken
prisoner on their own
planet, alluding to their
sense of the complexities
of American life.

"Can our truth-seekers lead us to the place where we are superhuman—shedding our Black bodies of institutional 'isms'?"

Lola Flash, AFROFUTURISM

Maj. Fannie Griffin McClendon (Ret.),
2022
Michael A. McCoy
–

Major Fannie Griffin McClendon served during World War II in the Women's Army Corps' 6888th Central Postal Directory Battalion—the only unit of African American women to serve abroad during the war. Under the leadership of Major Charity Adams, the "Six Triple Eight" was tasked with sorting and routing millions of pieces of mail intended for U.S. personnel in Europe. After the war, McClendon joined the Air Force and later became the first female commander of an all-male squadron with the strategic air command.

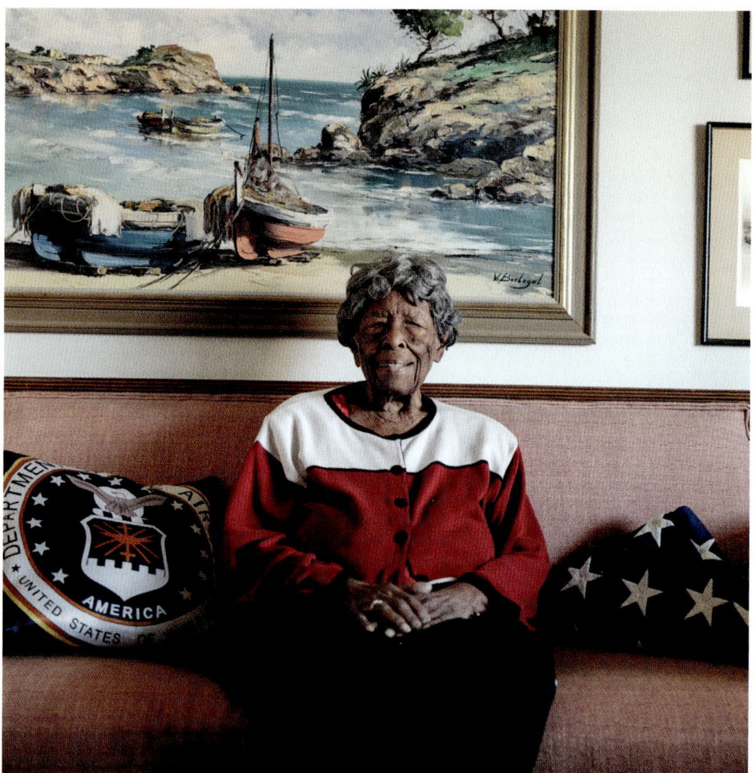

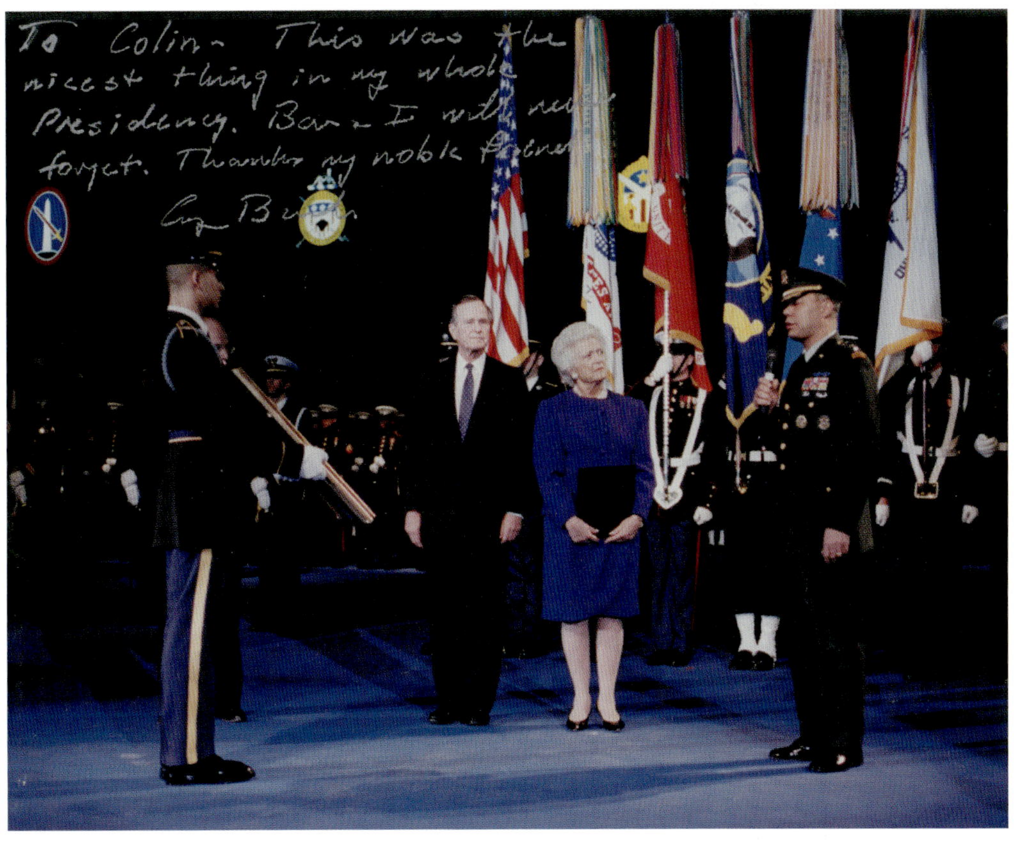

**Gen. Colin Powell's
swearing in as chairman
of the Joint Chiefs of Staff**,
1989; inscribed later
Unidentified photographer

The Past, 2019
From the series
My America
Rashod Taylor

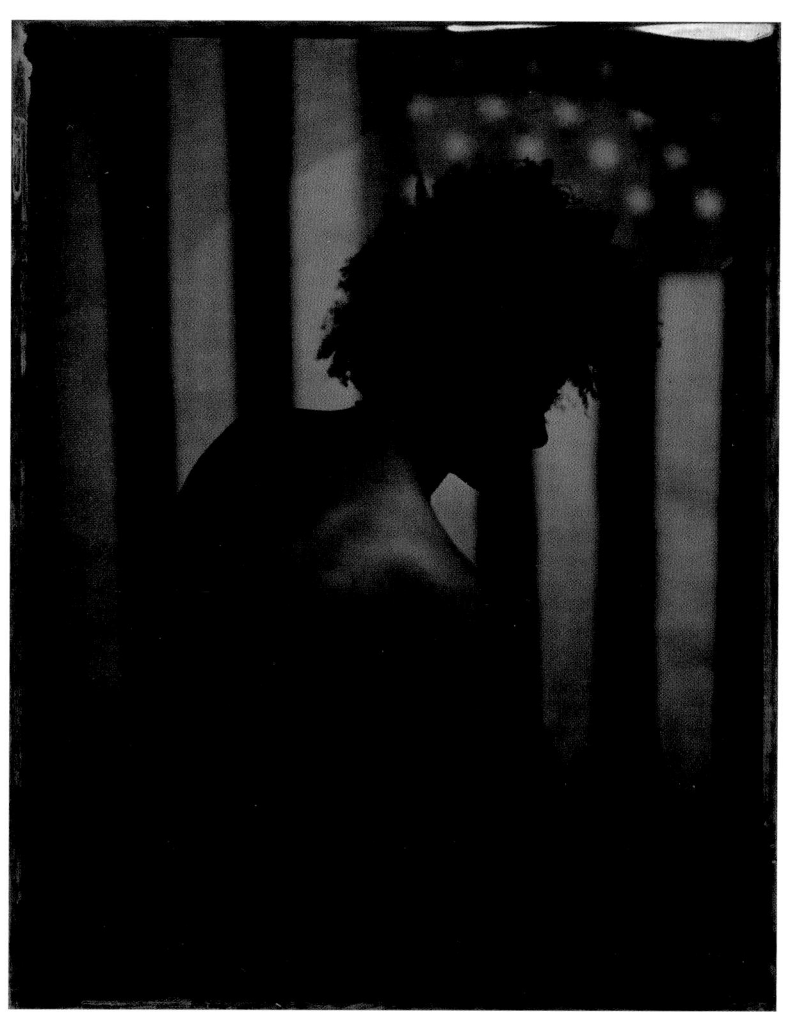

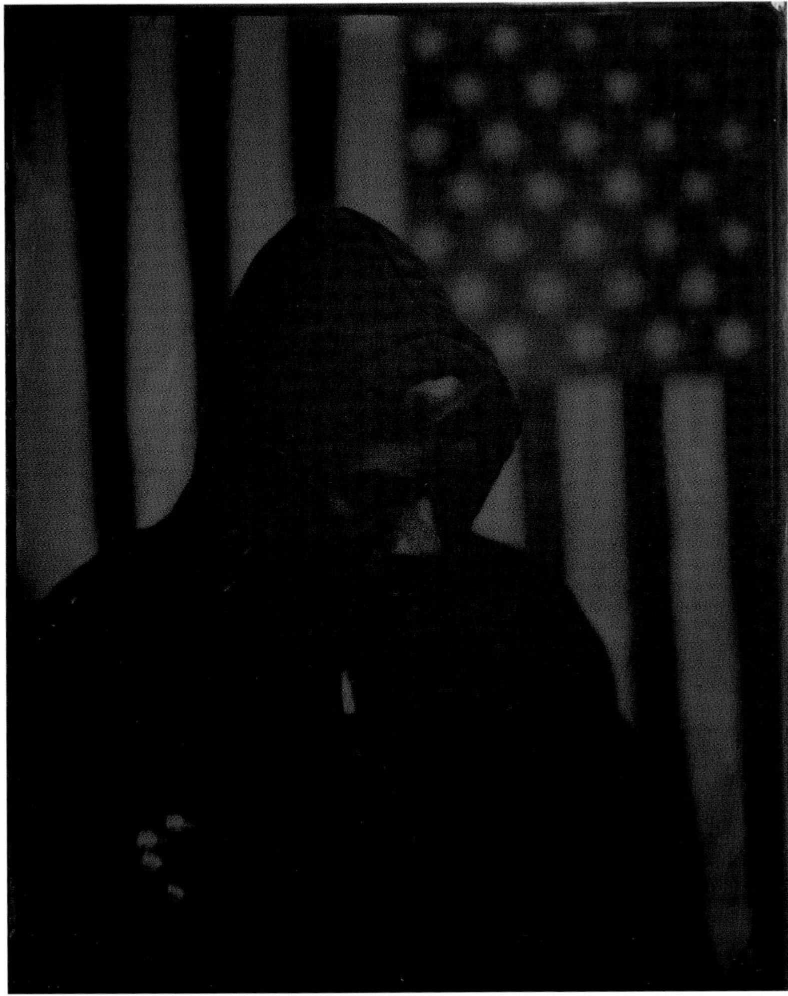

The Present, 2018
From the series
My America
Rashod Taylor

—

Rashod Taylor's *My America* is a series of contemporary tintypes created through vintage methods. The series explores history's ongoing presence and influence on present-day lives. Using a wet-plate collodion process that dates to the 1850s, the antique appearance of Taylor's images invite viewers to reflect on the history of race and the paradox of freedom in America.

Josephine Sampson,
1910s
Charles E. Kerfoot
–

The flag is a collective portrait, in the same way these five photographs form a collective image of the sitter, Josephine Sampson. Sampson inscribed this series of posed photographs to her sisters. Centered among other props, the U.S. flag is liberated from an elevated, monumental state. Instead, it exists alongside a graduation mortarboard and frilly cartwheel hat in one of many passport-photo–sized images Sampson selects to signal personal achievement, attentive self-fashioning, and national belonging.

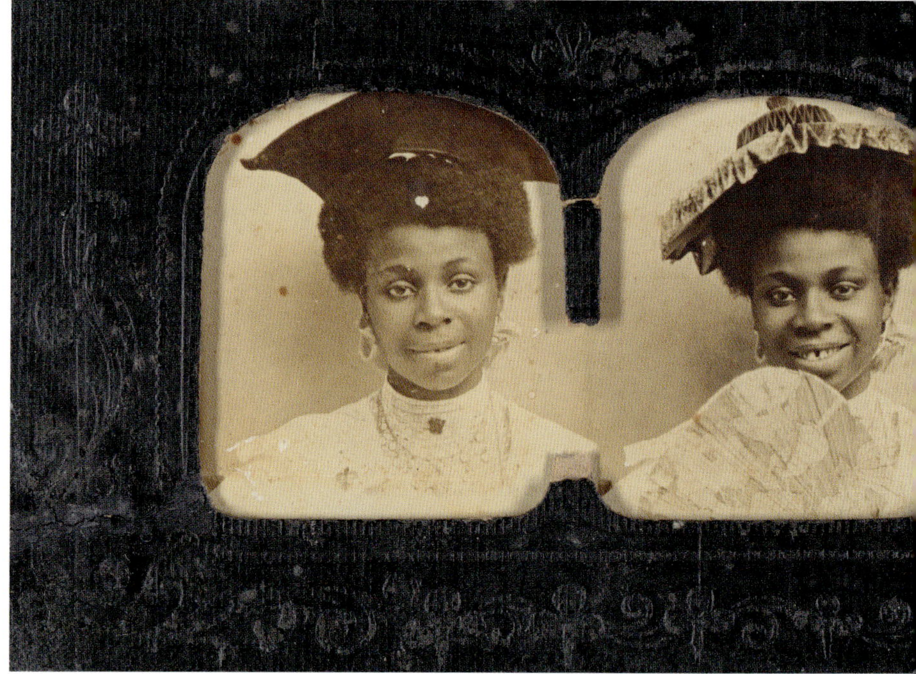

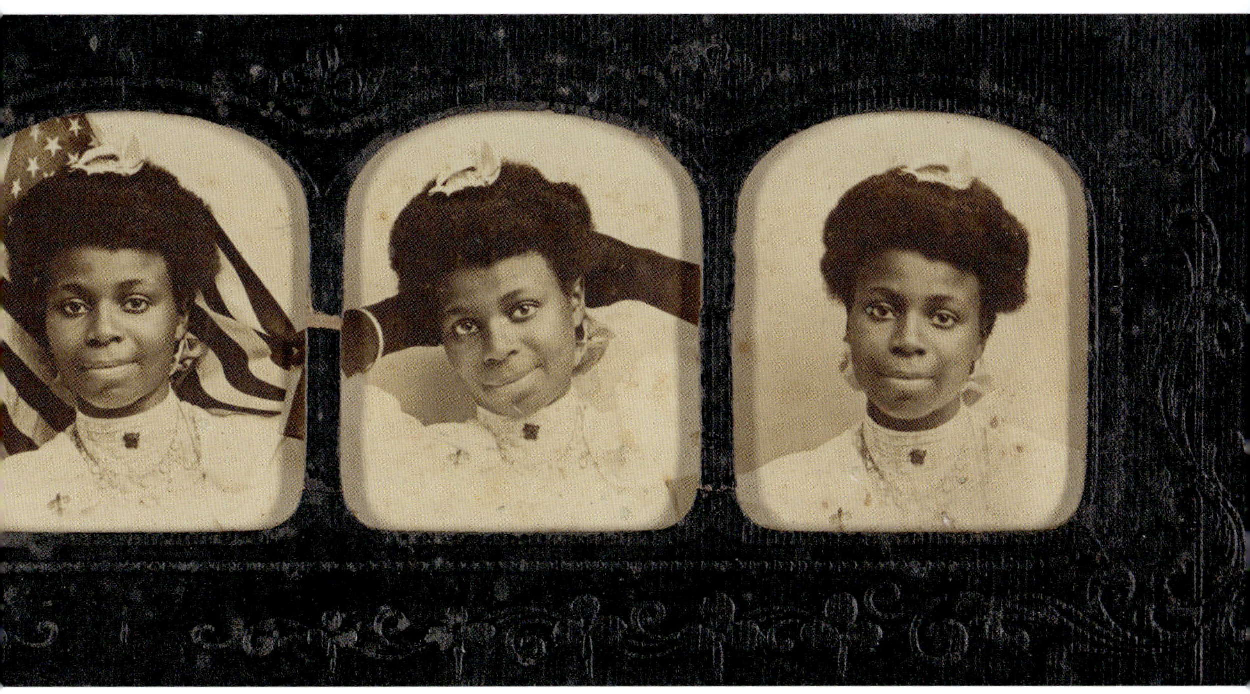

United States Air Force Honor Guard Pallbearers Carry the Flag-Draped Coffin of U.S. Air Force Four Star General Daniel "Chappie" James from an Air Force C-141 Starlifter Airplane at Andrews Air Force Base, Suitland, Maryland, February 26, 1978
Milton Williams

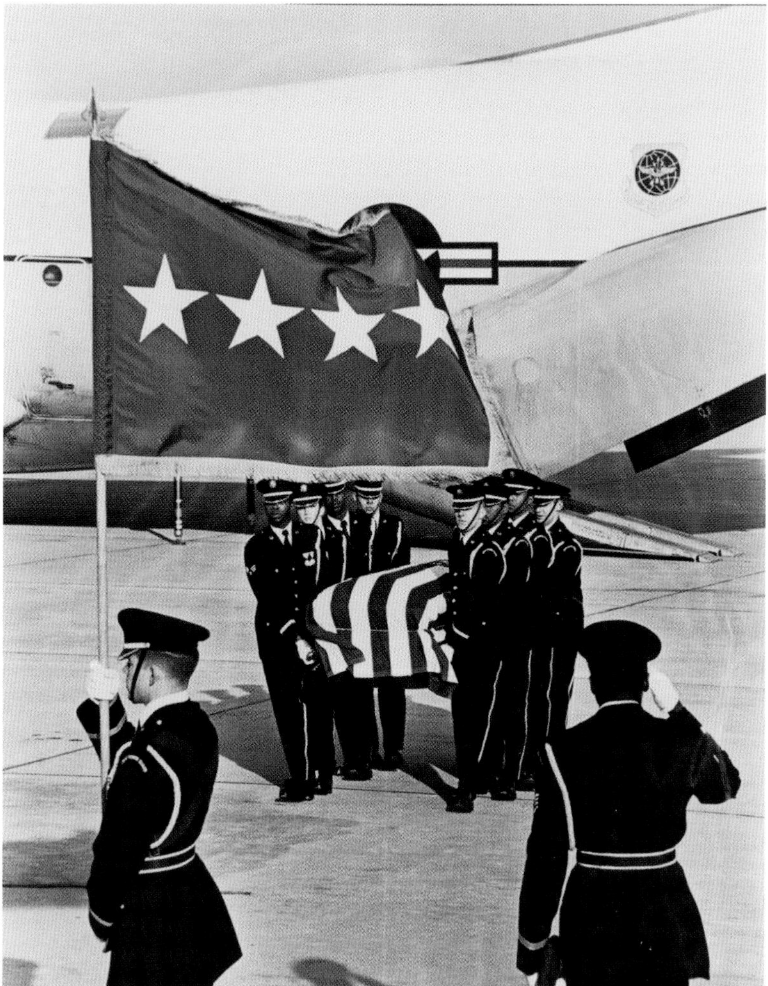

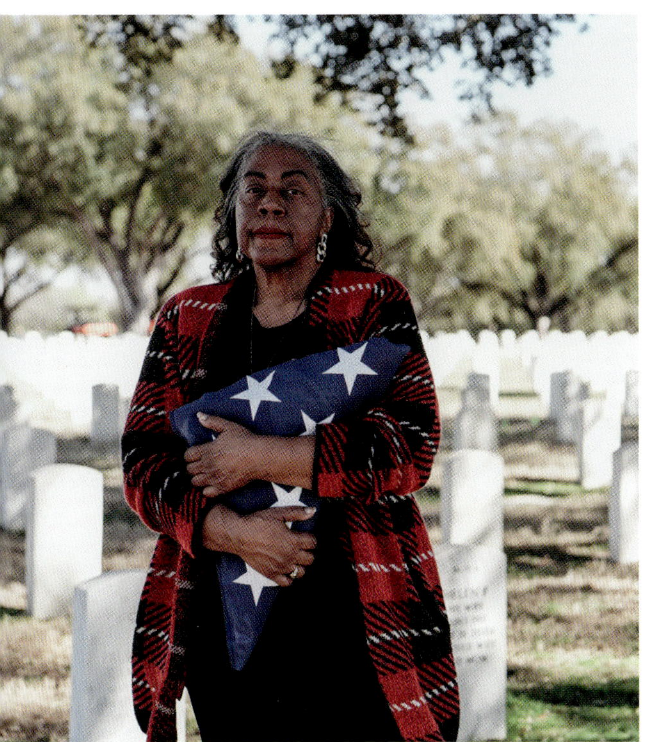

Angela Holder holding a folded flag at a ceremony honoring her great–uncle Cpl. Jesse Moore, 2024
Michael A. McCoy

—

In August 1917, following the arrest and assault of Black officers stationed at Camp Logan in Houston, Texas, 156 Black soldiers from the 24th Infantry Regiment there took up arms. They marched to the city's San Felipe district in response to racial tensions and ongoing police brutality. In a violent confrontation between the soldiers and law enforcement, five soldiers, five police officers, and eleven civilians died. After three courts-martial, in the largest murder trial in U.S. history, 118 soldiers were tried, 110 were convicted with no appeal, 19 were executed, and 63 were sentenced to life in prison. More than 100 years later, in November 2023, the Army overturned all 110 convictions and acknowledged that the soldiers had not received fair trials. Angela Holder's great-uncle Cpl. Jesse Moore was one of the 19 men hanged for his participation in the riot. She holds the burial flag that was presented to her during a memorial ceremony at Fort Sam Houston National Cemetery in February 2024, where new headstones honoring the executed soldiers were unveiled.

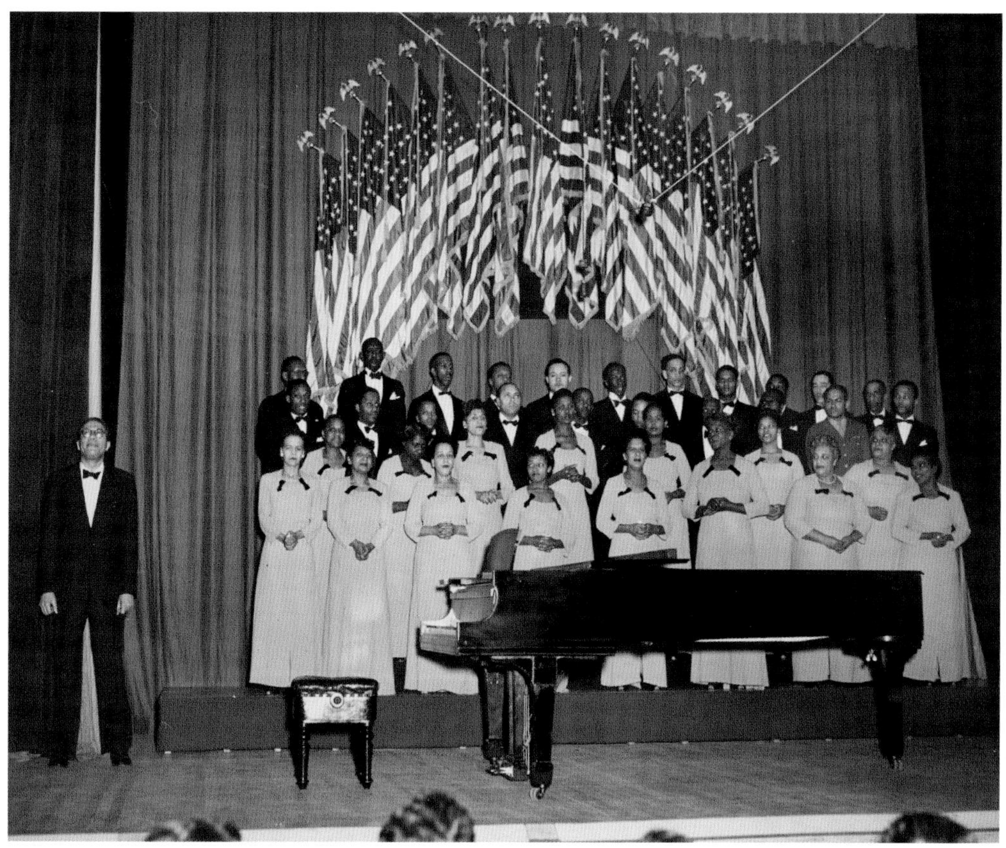

**The Hall Johnson
Choir**, ca. 1935–52
Raymond K. Martin

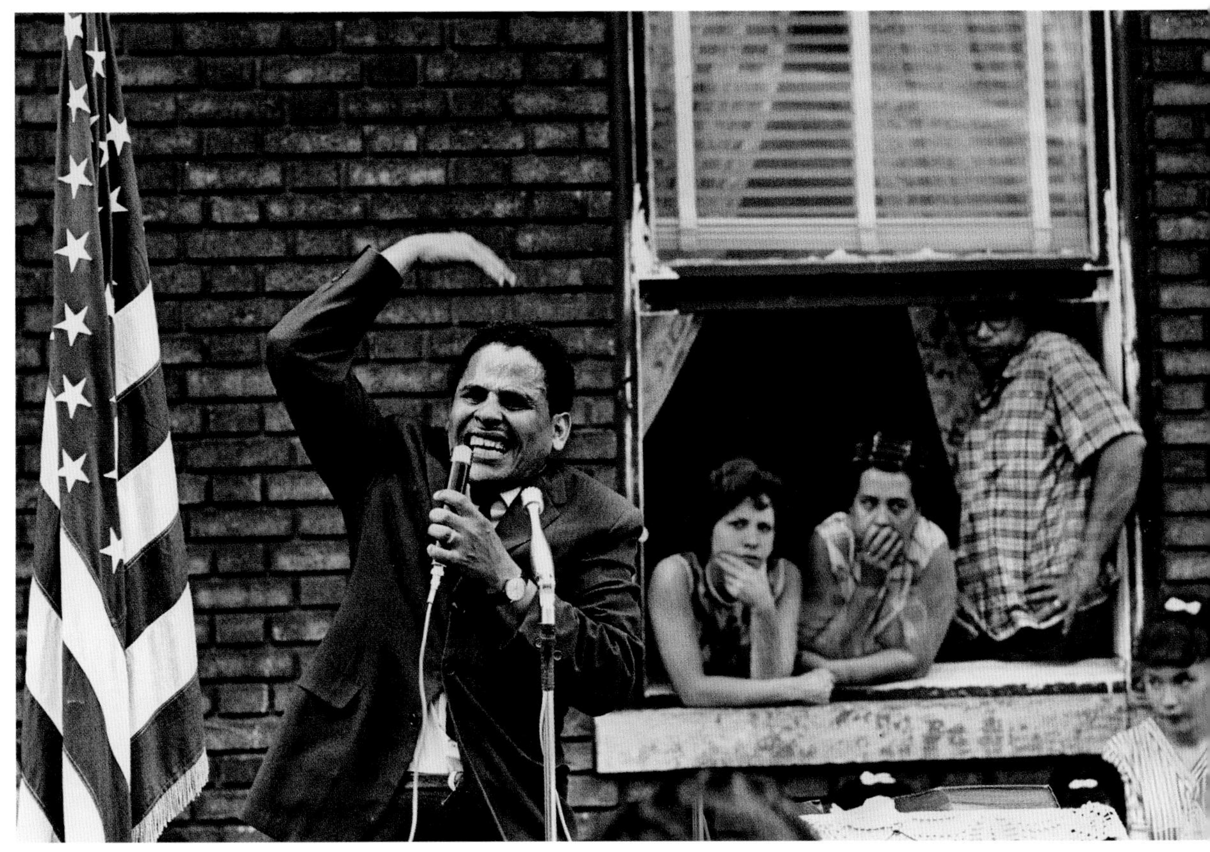

El Ministro, 1964; printed later
From the series **The Puerto Rican
Diaspora Documentary Project**
Frank Espada

Girls of the Booker Washington School, Tuskegee, Ala.—Mrs. McKinley in Near Carriage, 1899
Strohmeyer & Wyman

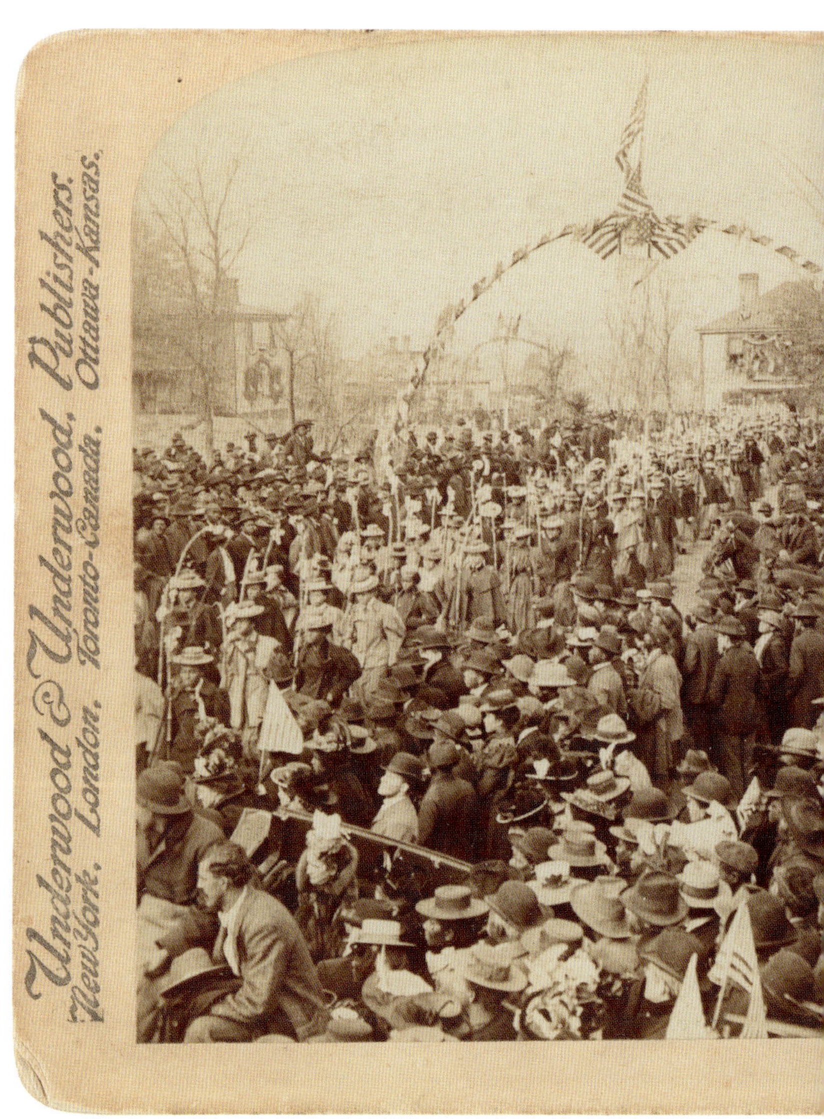

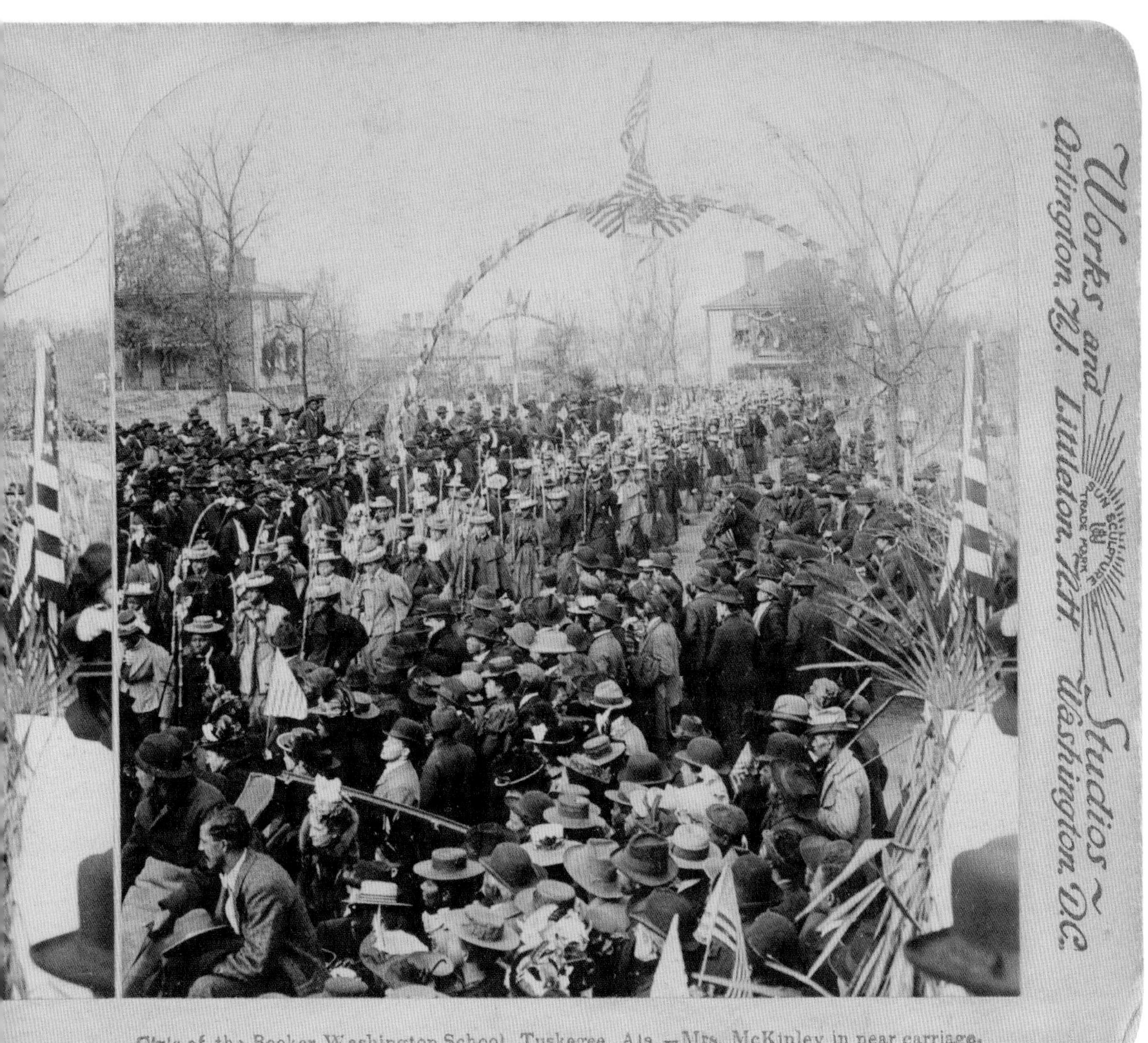

Girls of the Booker Washington School. Tuskegee, Ala.—Mrs. McKinley in near carriage.
Copyright 1899 by Strohmeyer & Wyman.

Father with child at Baltimore's AFRAM Festival, 2017
Michael A. McCoy

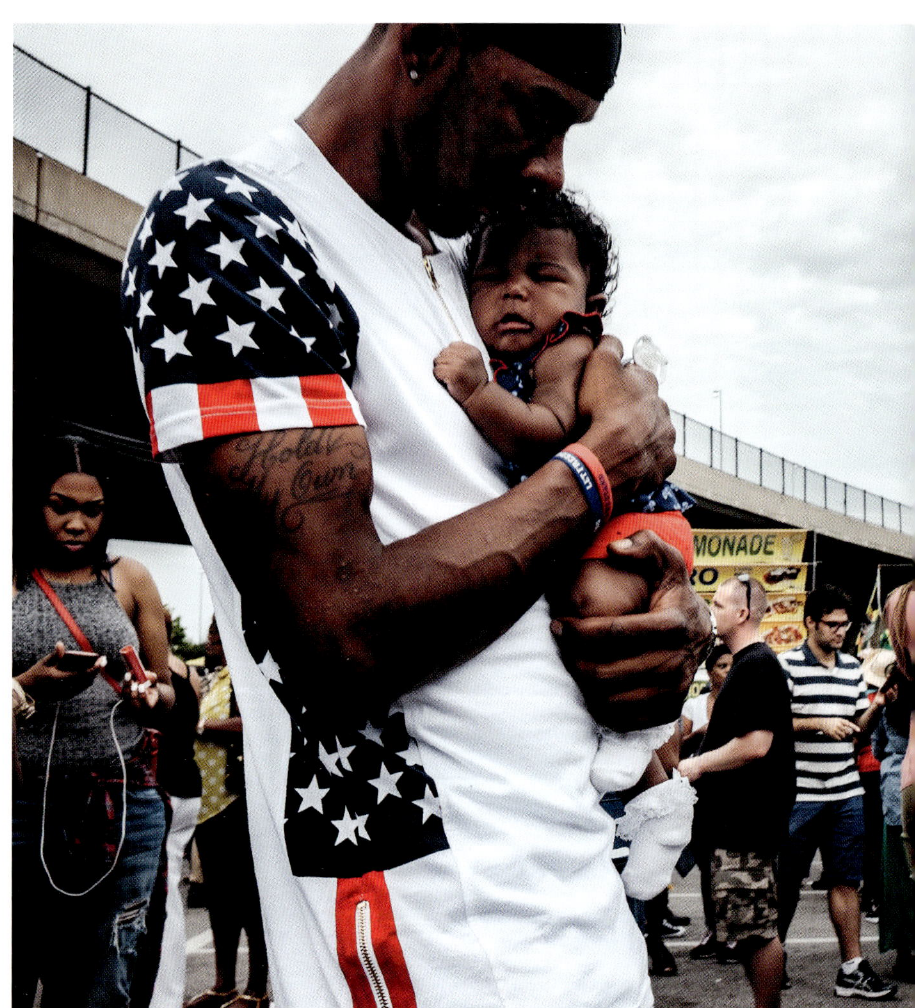

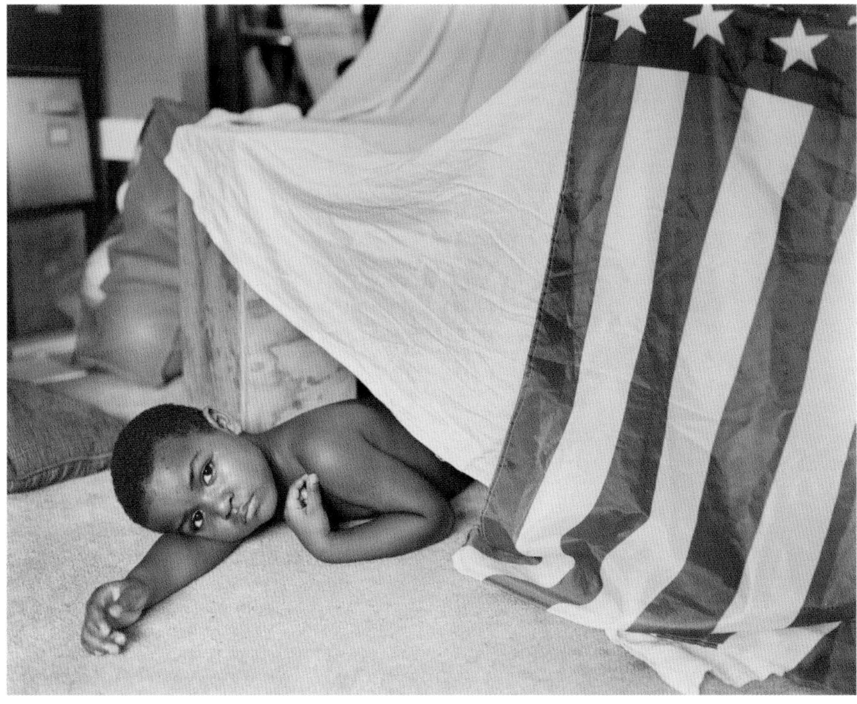

LJ and His Fort, 2020
From the series
Little Black Boy
Rashod Taylor

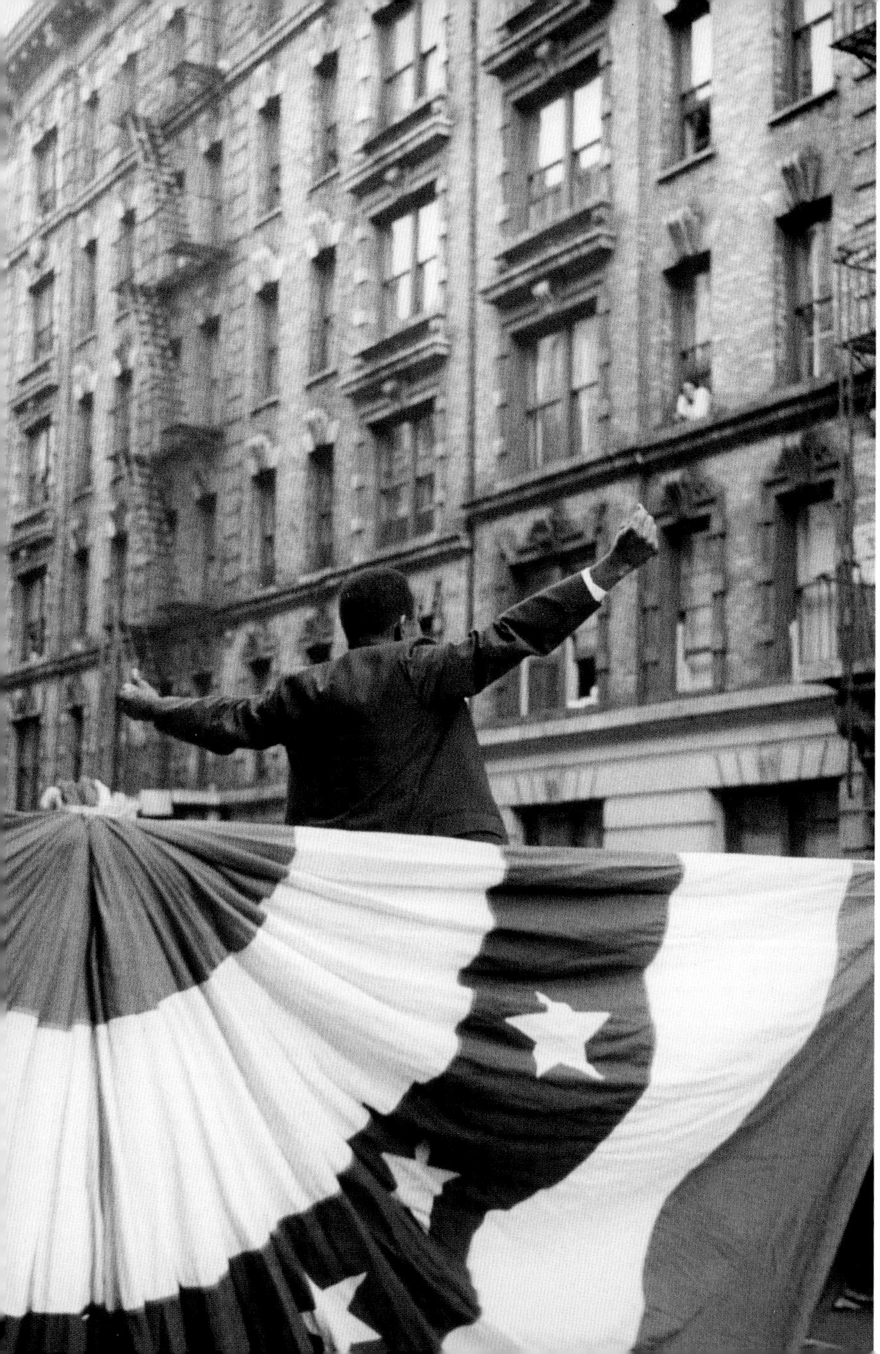

Harlem, New York •
USA, 1963
Leonard Freed

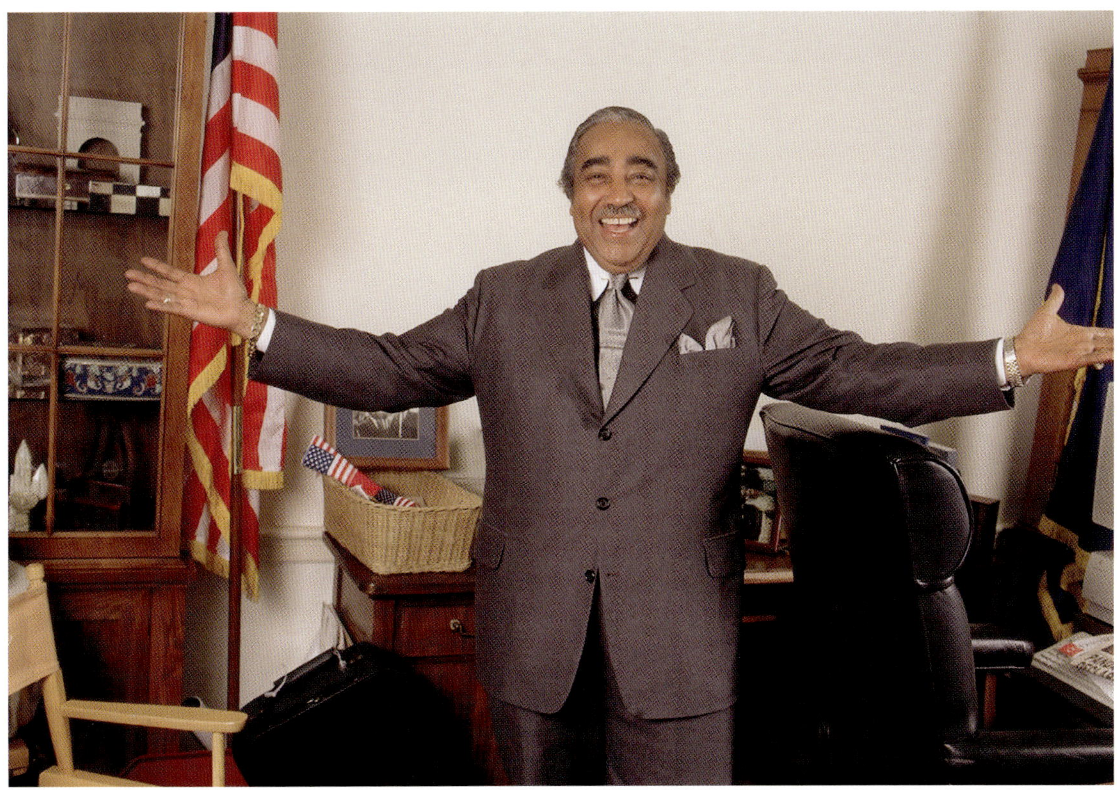

Congressman Charles Rangel in his office, 1998
Frederick Watkins Jr.

Shanae Rowland, Age 21, American, 2008; printed 2024
From the series
Young Americans
Sheila Pree Bright

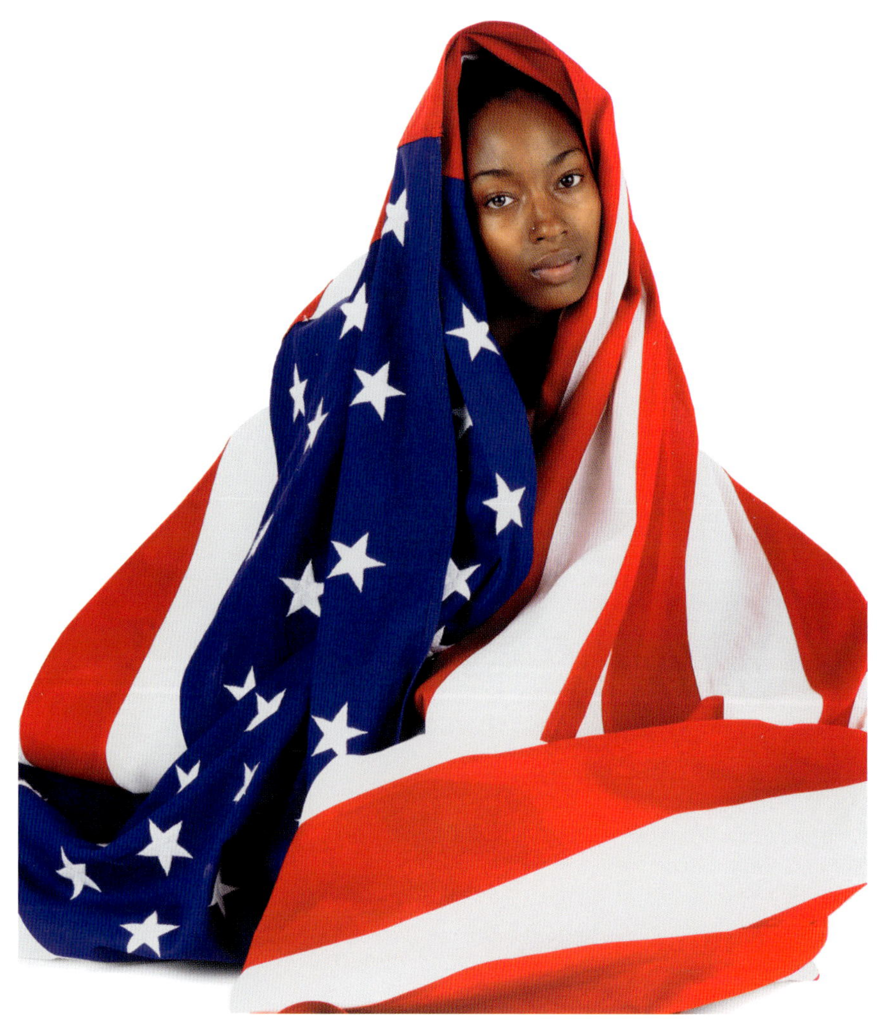

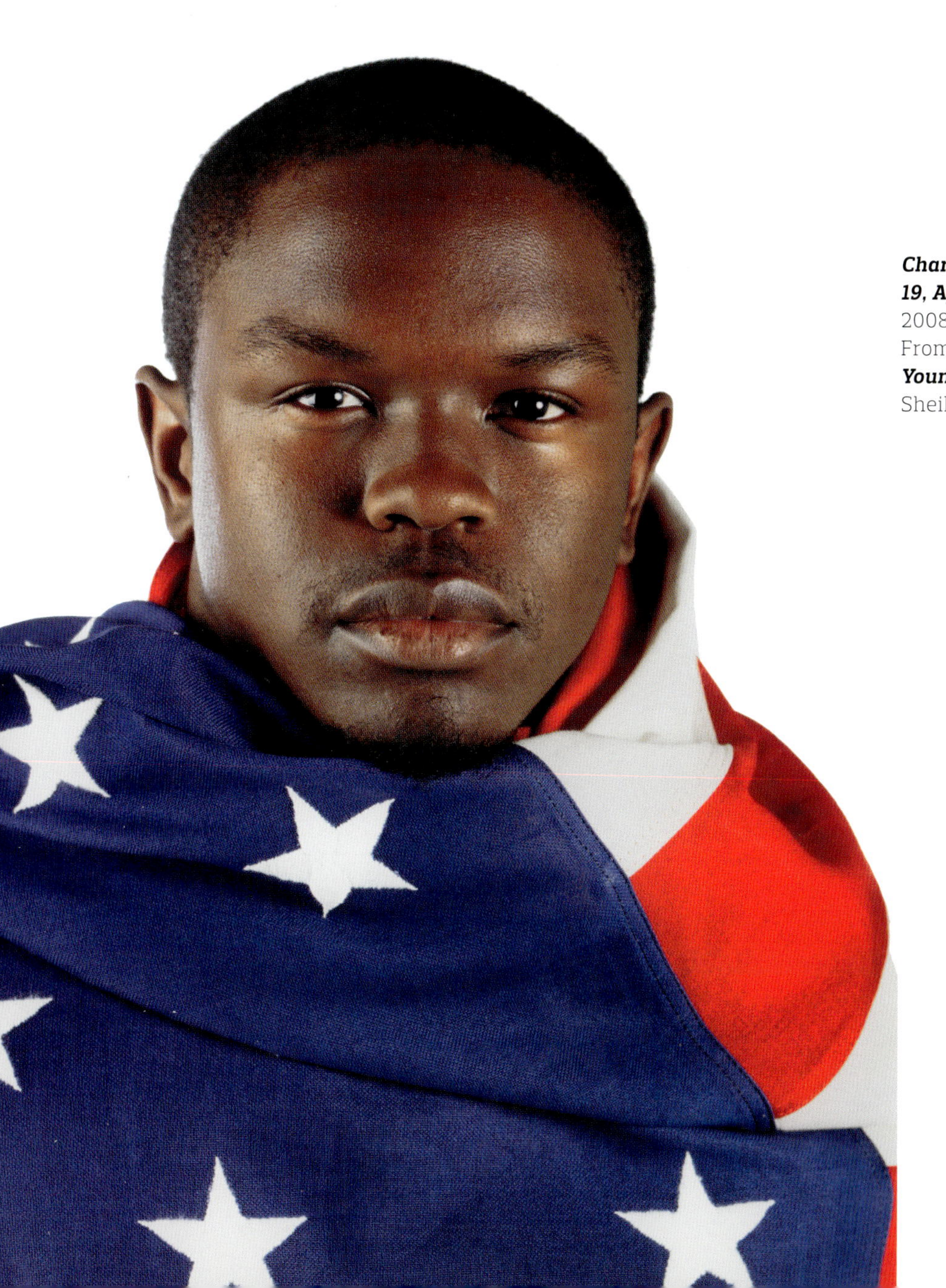

Charles Cauthen, Age 19, African American, 2008; printed 2024
From the series
Young Americans
Sheila Pree Bright

"Being an African American makes me feel proud because of those that came before and fought for my freedom."

Shanae Rowland

"Home, a place where I'm comfortable."

Charles Cauthen

Wheatpasted photograph of Shanae Rowland on the side of a stairwell, Coconut Grove Neighborhood, Miami, Florida, 2008
Sheila Pree Bright

—

Young Americans, a series of photographs by Sheila Pree Bright, explores the national identities of millennials, those born between 1983 and 2000. In 2006, Bright invited a racially, ethnically, politically, and geographically varied group of young people to pose with the American flag in ways that expressed their feelings about the country. The sitters were photographed draped in the flag, embracing it as if it was part of their person, conveying a sense of comfort, hopefulness, and longing. Bright then asked participants to self-identify and name their identities. Shanae (left) identified as "American," while Charles identified as "African American."

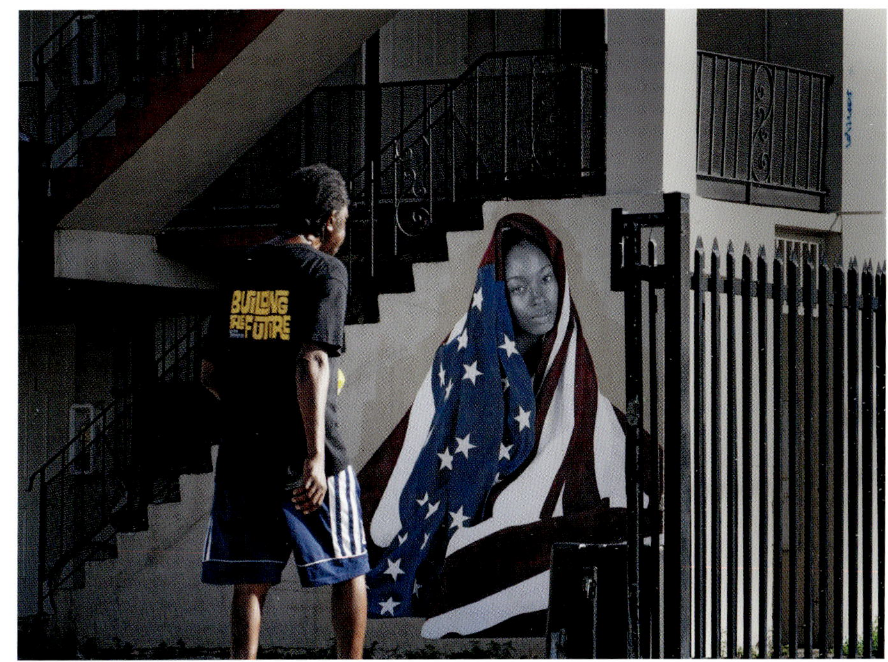

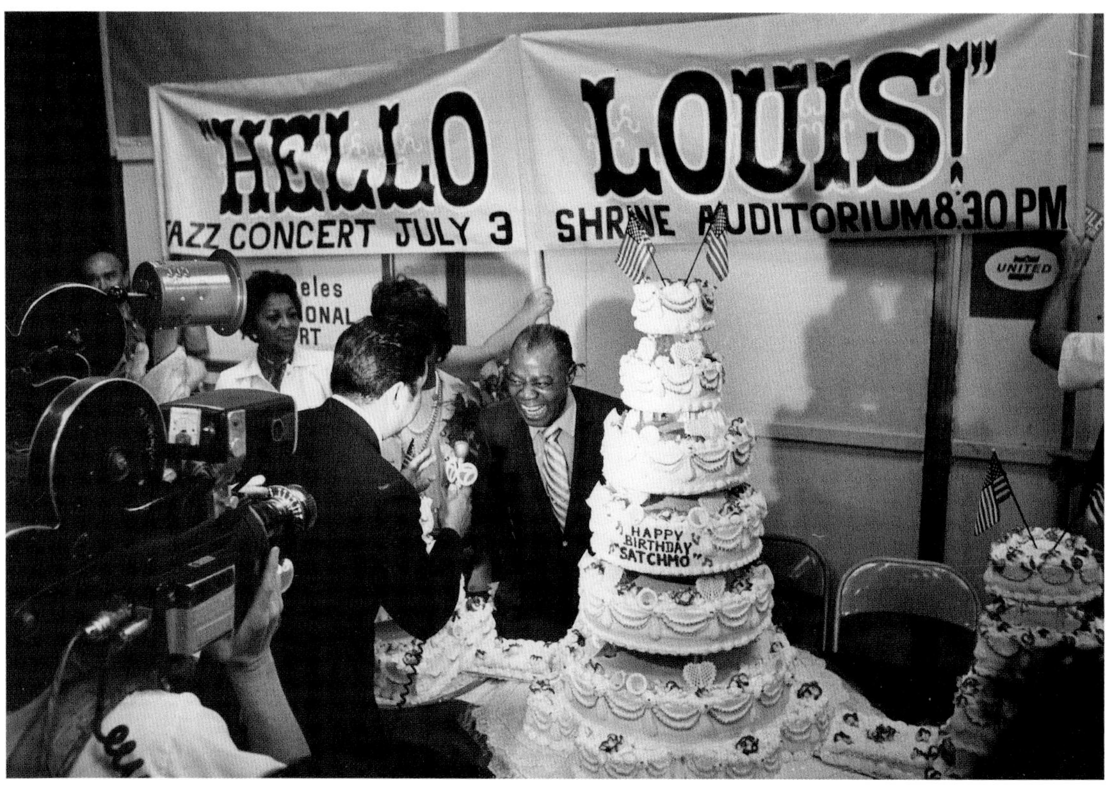

Louis Armstrong's 70th birthday celebration at the Shrine Auditorium, Los Angeles, California, July 1970
Moneta Sleet Jr.

—

In his autobiography, Louis Armstrong described his birthday as July 4, 1900, aligning his birth with Independence Day and the start of the twentieth century.

James Brown and Bootsy Collins perform during Brown's "Living in America" television concert, Los Angeles, California, June 1991
James L. Mitchell

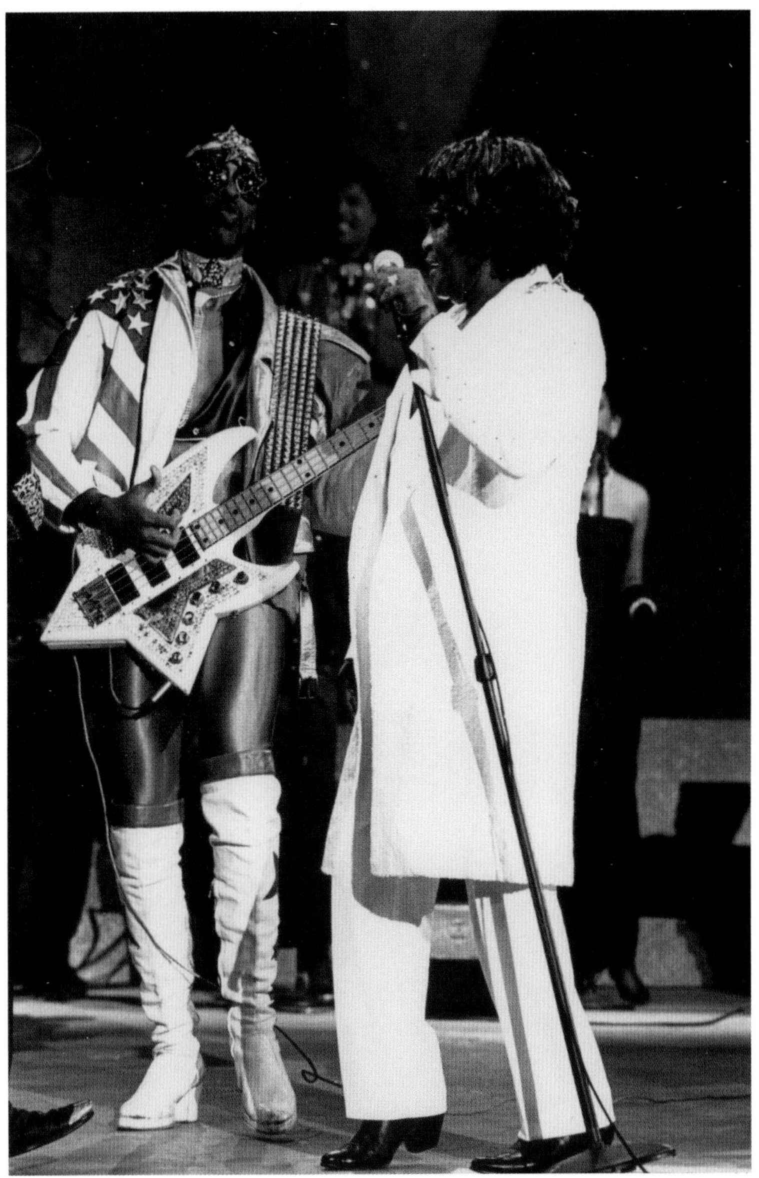

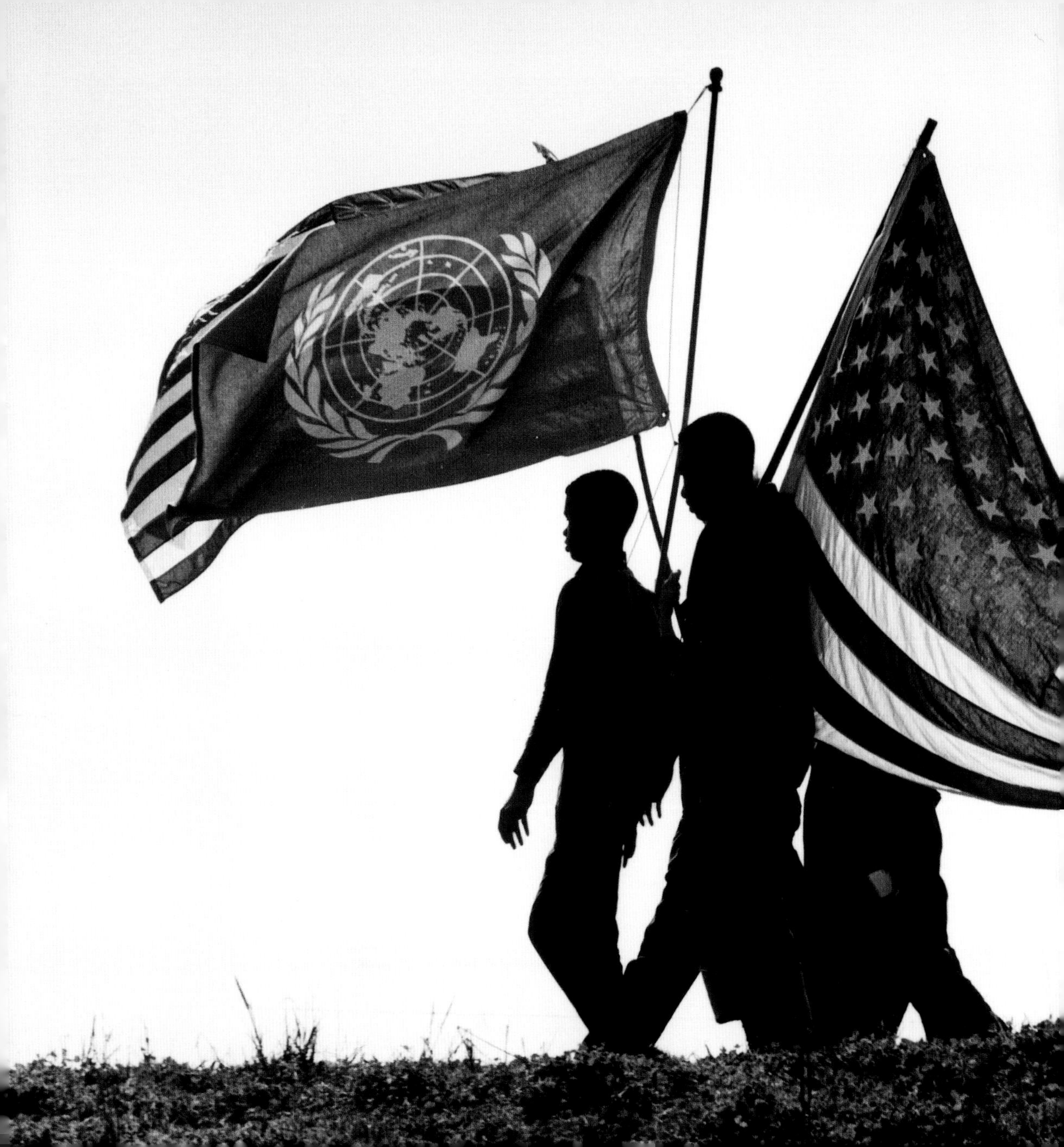

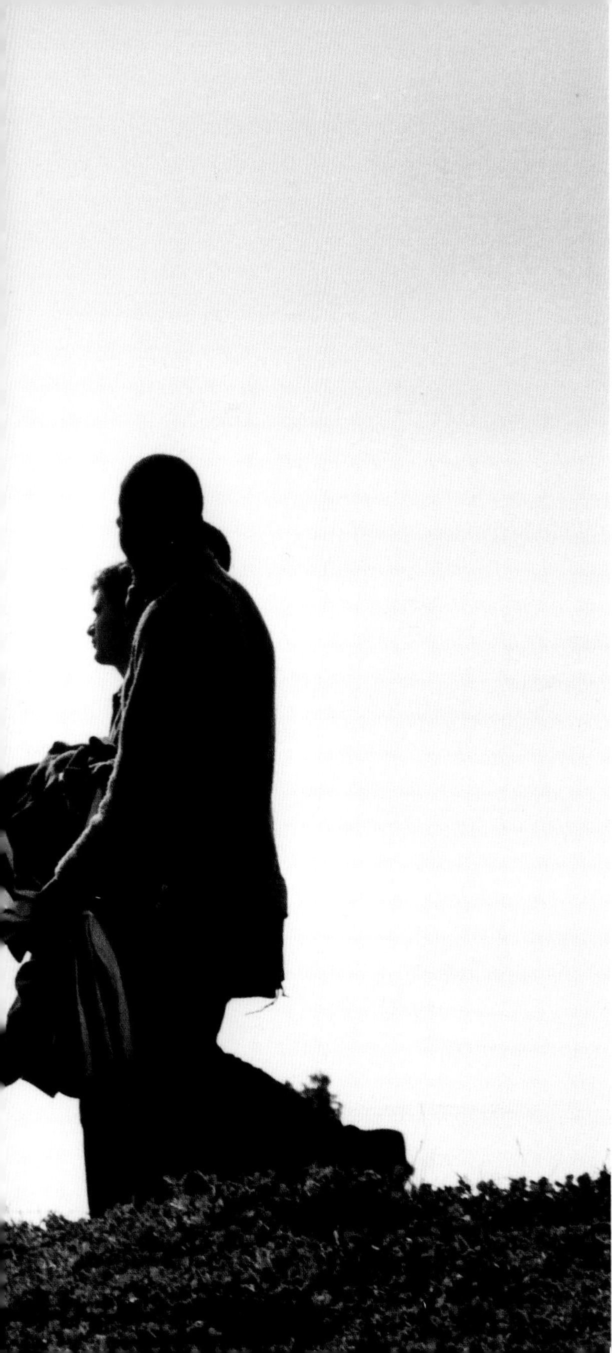

Flag-Bearing Marchers, Selma to Montgomery March, 1965
James H. Karales

The March on Washington, August 28, 1963;
printed ca. 2021
James P. Blair

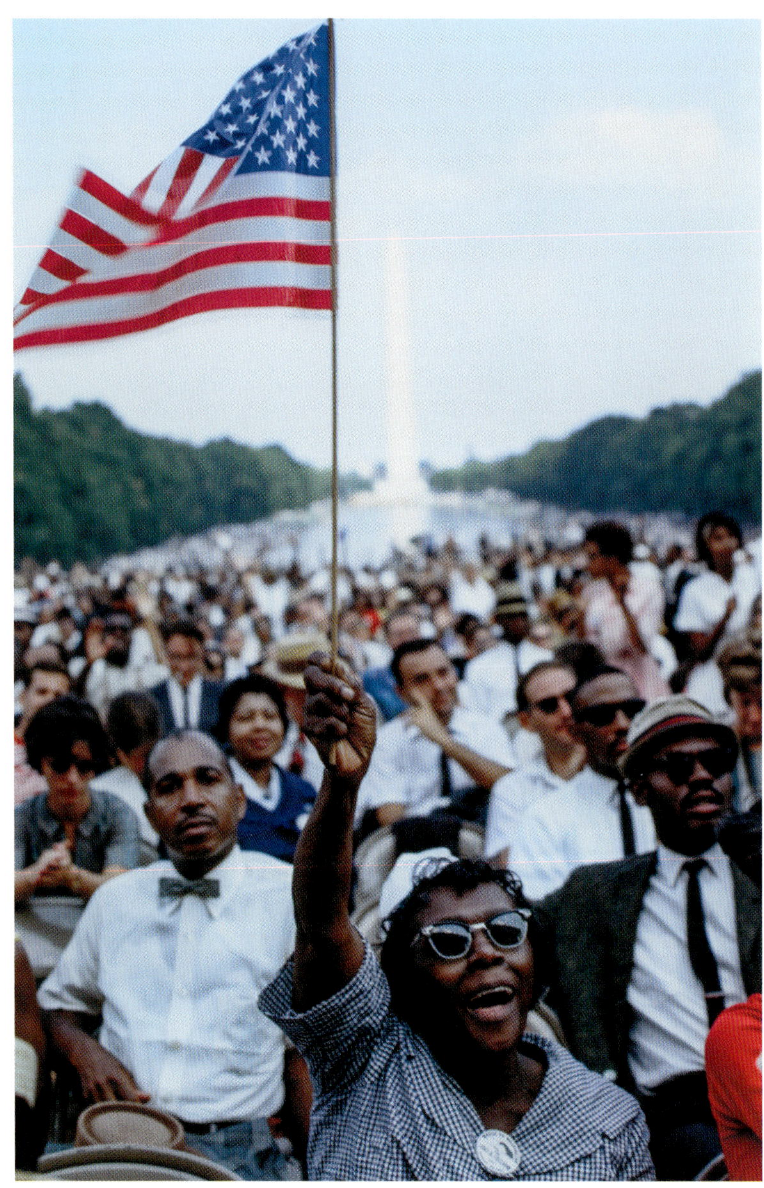

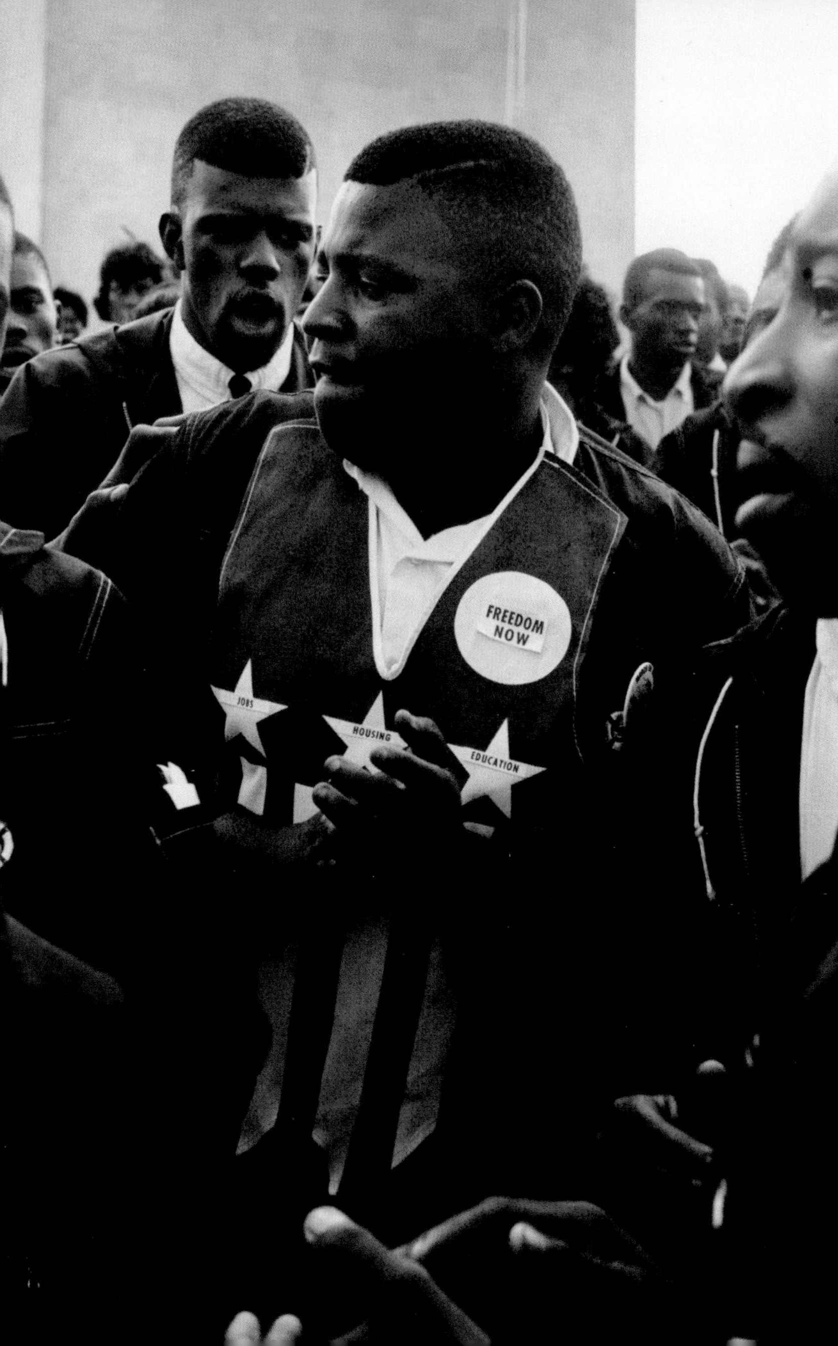

A participant during the March on Washington, August 28, 1963; printed 2013
Leonard Freed

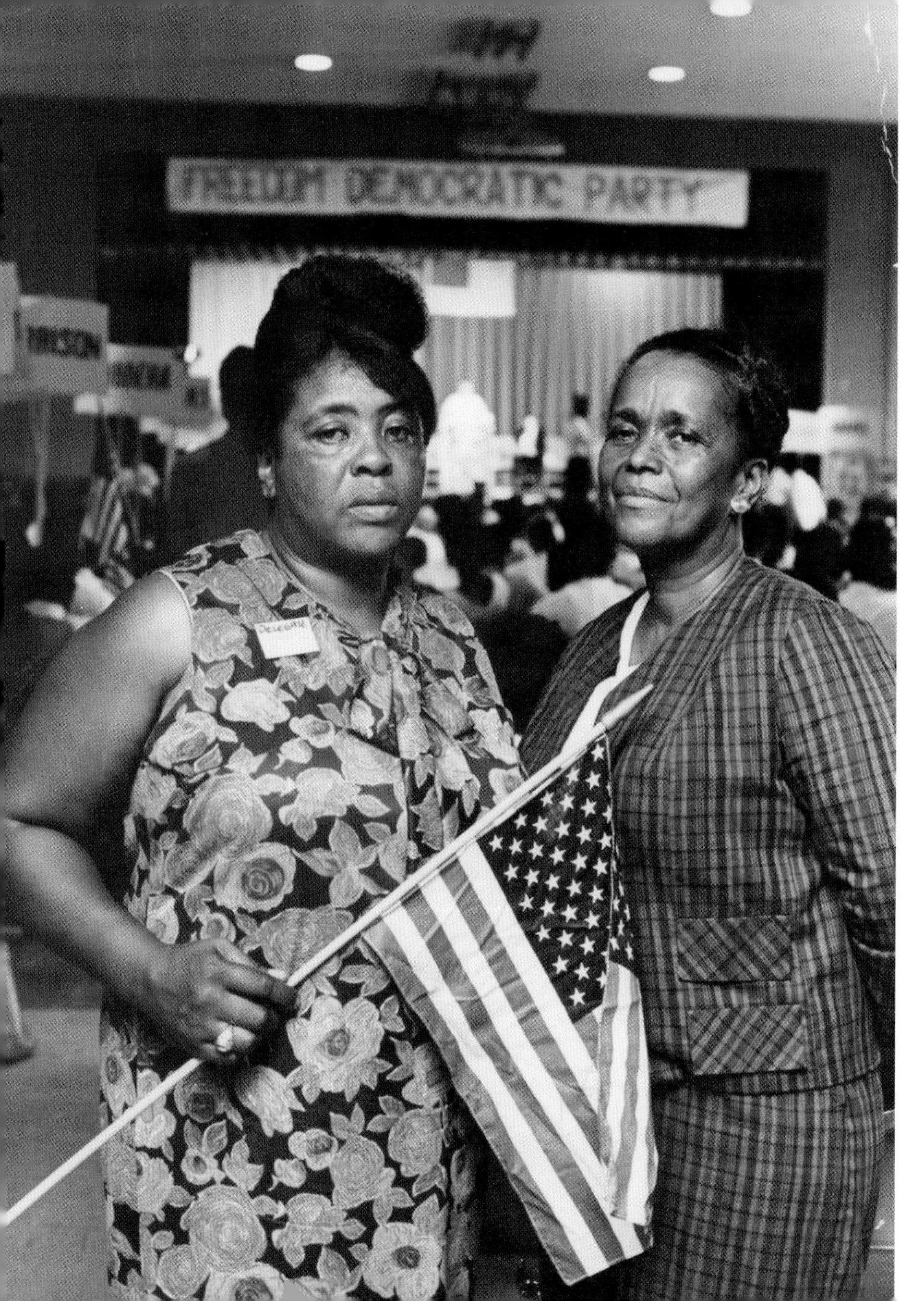

FREEDOM DEMOCRATIC PARTY

Fannie Lou Hamer and Ella Baker at the Mississippi Freedom Democratic Party Convention, Jackson, Mississippi, August 1964
Maurice Sorrell
—

Fannie Lou Hamer and Ella Baker helped organize the Mississippi Freedom Summer, which brought hundreds of Black and white students to the South to help with voter registration. Months later, Hamer and Baker founded the Mississippi Freedom Democratic Party in 1964 (see pp. 10–12). Baker, who held key roles with the National Association for the Advancement of Colored People and the Southern Christian Leadership Conference (SCLC) in Mississippi, was a strong promoter of grassroots organizing. In 1960, she convinced the SCLC to convene college students from around the South at Shaw University in North Carolina, where they founded the Student Nonviolent Coordinating Committee (SNCC). The same year, SNCC partnered with the Congress of Racial Equality to organize the Freedom Rides. An inspiring teacher and mentor, Baker helped to train future leaders of the movement, including Julian Bond, Diane Nash, Stokely Carmichael, Bob Moses, and Bernice Johnson Reagon.

"Nobody's free until everybody's free."

Fannie Lou Hamer

"Give light, and people will find the way."

Ella Baker

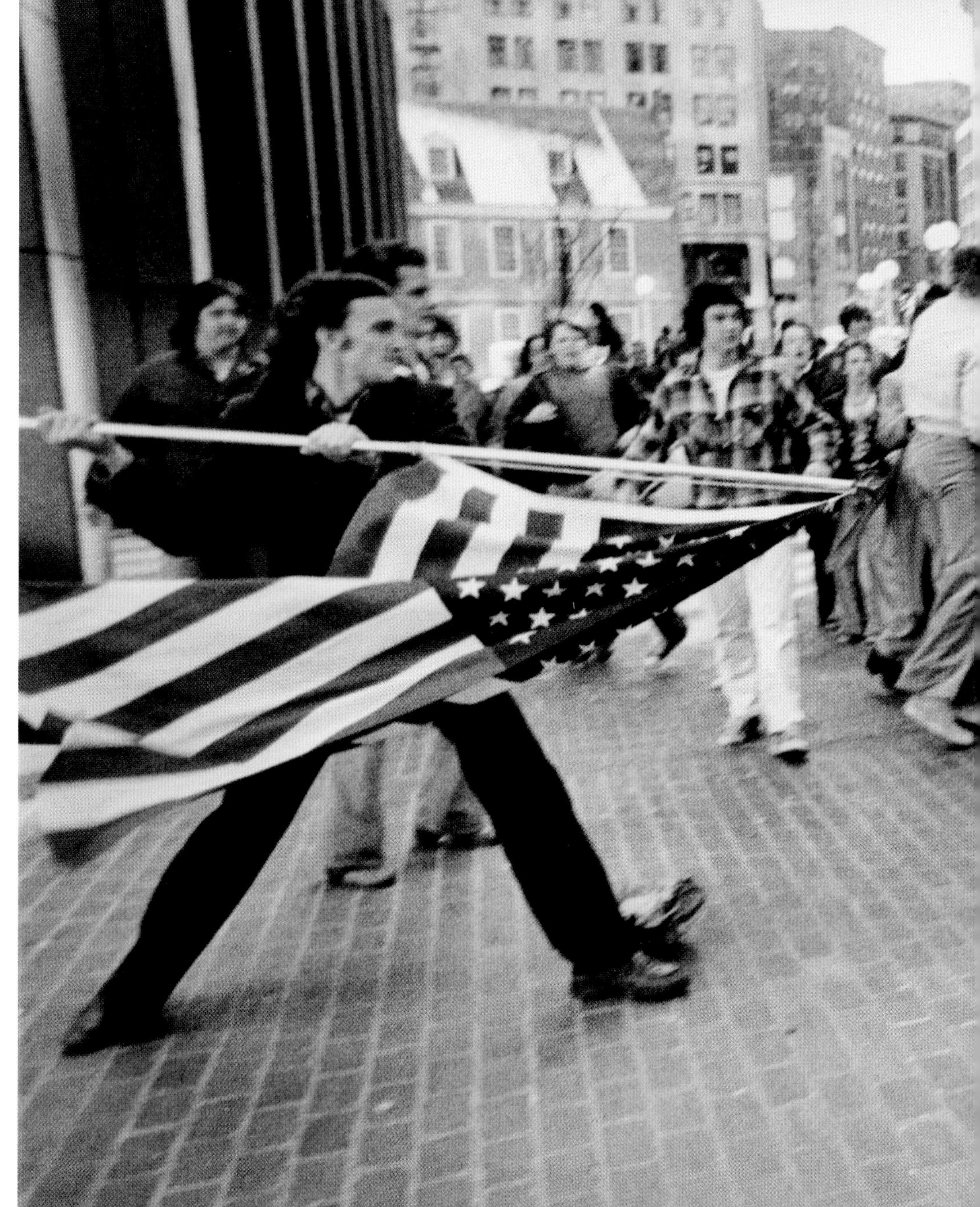

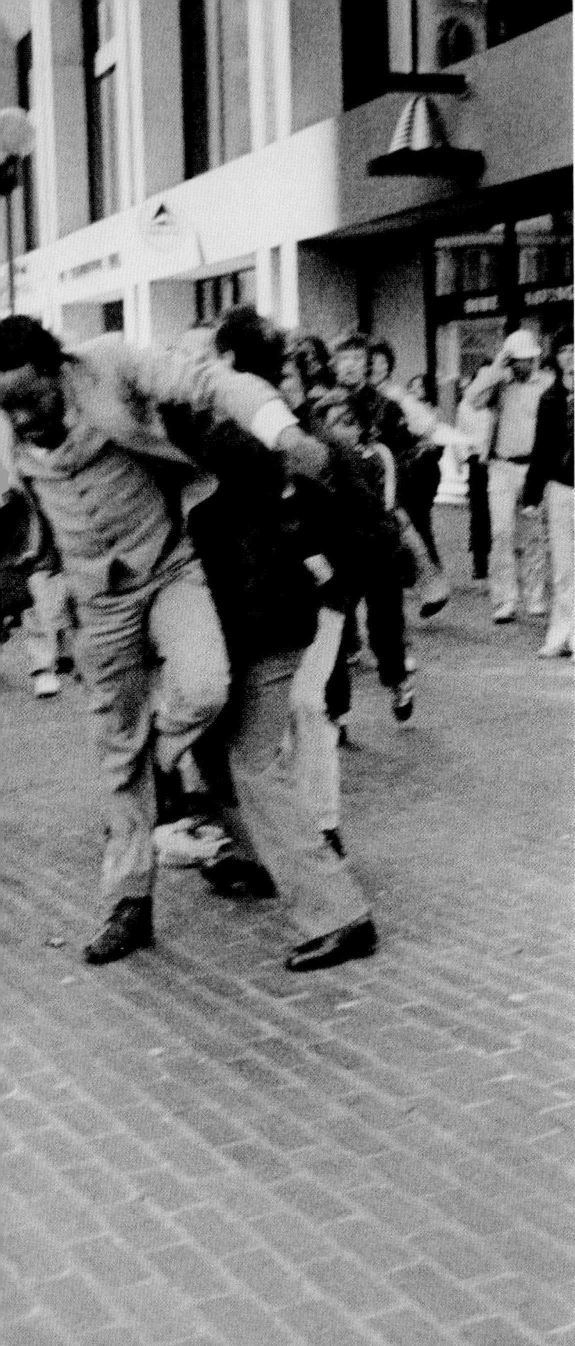

***The Soiling of Old
Glory***, April 5, 1976
Stanley Forman

Protestors in Ferguson, Missouri,
October 11, 2014
From the series ***Black Love Matters***
Zun Lee
—

To create his series *Black Love Matters*, photographer Zun Lee spent time in Ferguson after the killing of eighteen-year-old Michael Brown by a police officer. According to Lee, his photography features images of "people whose struggle is often rendered invisible by the media frenzy." A focal point here is the upside-down flag, signifying the community's frustration over Brown's death and their anger at what they viewed as a never-ending cycle of disenfranchisement aimed at Black citizens. According to U.S. code, "The flag should never be displayed with the union down, except as a signal of dire distress in instances of extreme danger to life or property."

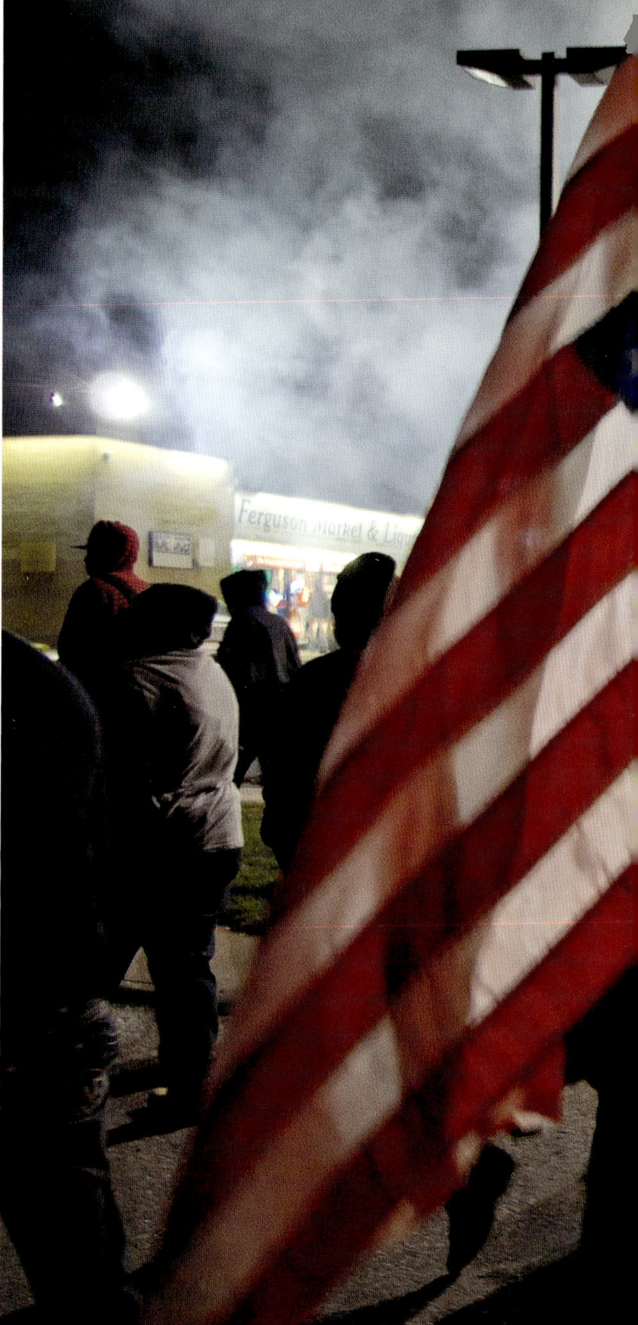

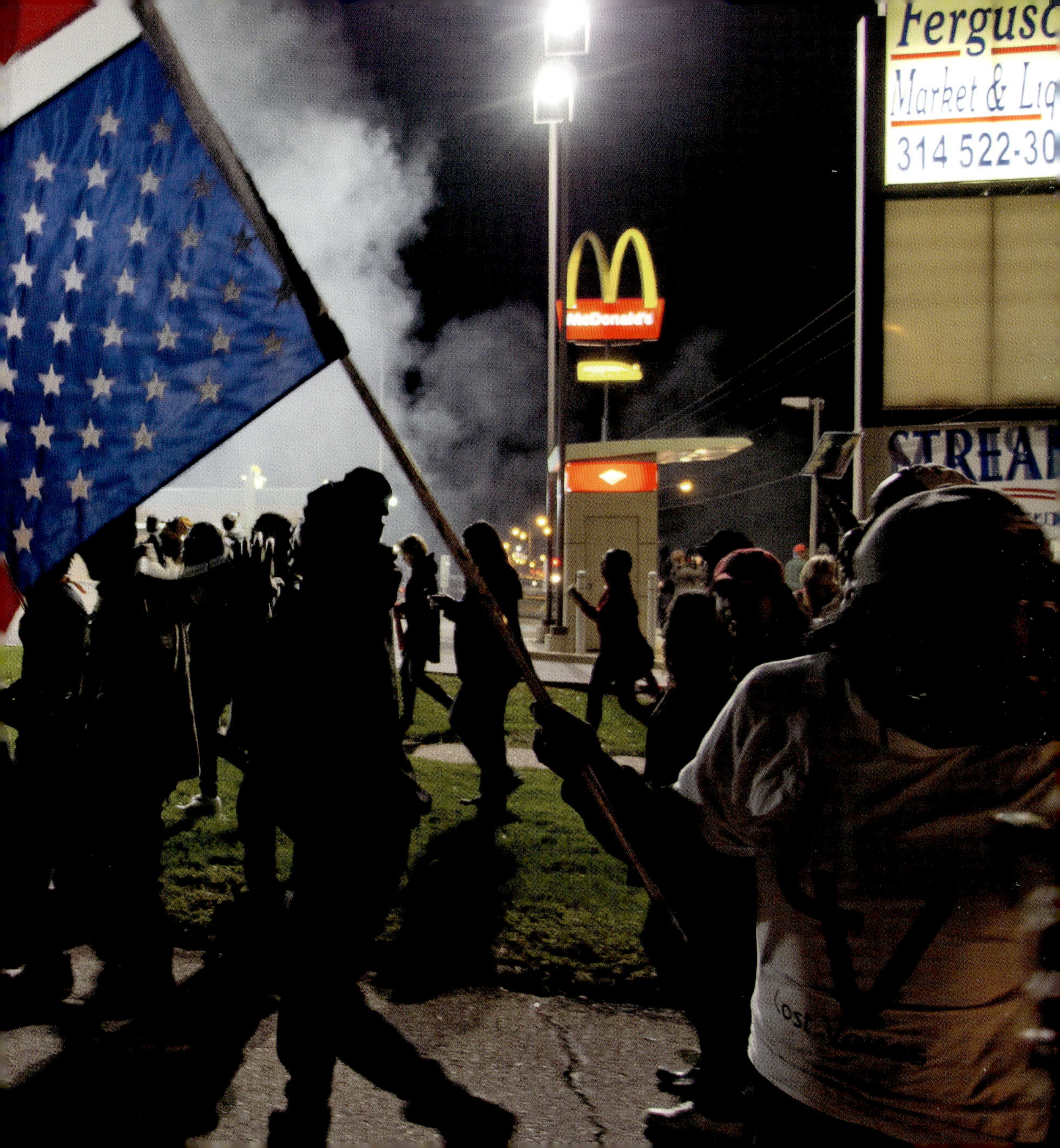

Fergus
Market & Liq
314 522-30
McDonald's
STREA

Glory, October 16, 1995
From the series
One Million Strong
Roderick Terry
—

A Civil War reenactor attending the Million Man March in Washington, D.C.

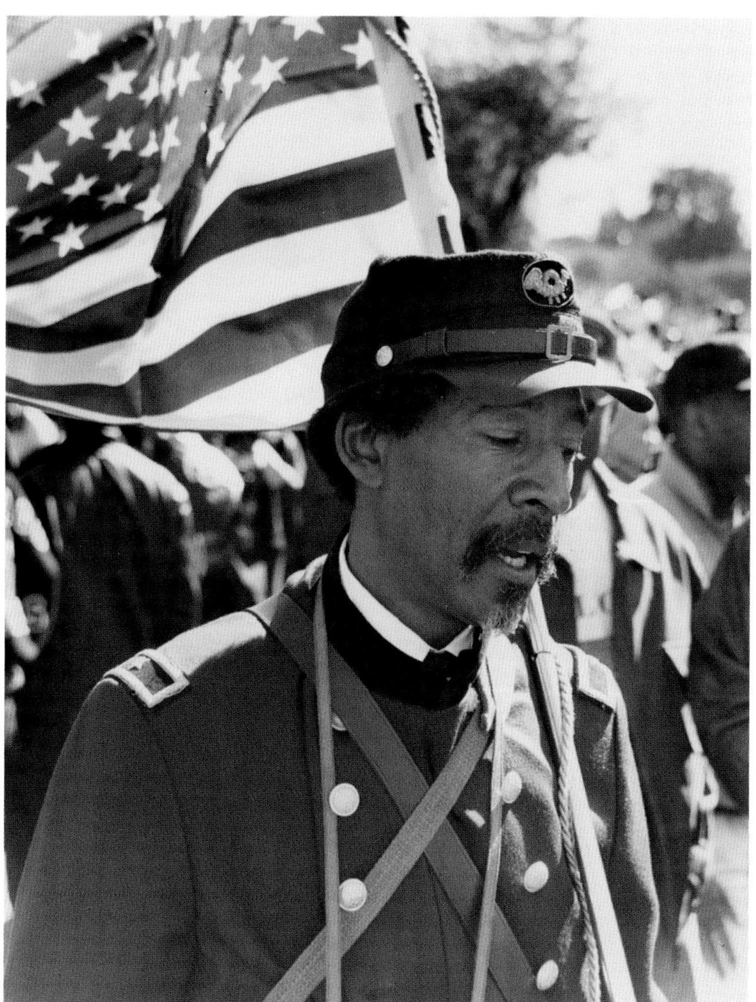

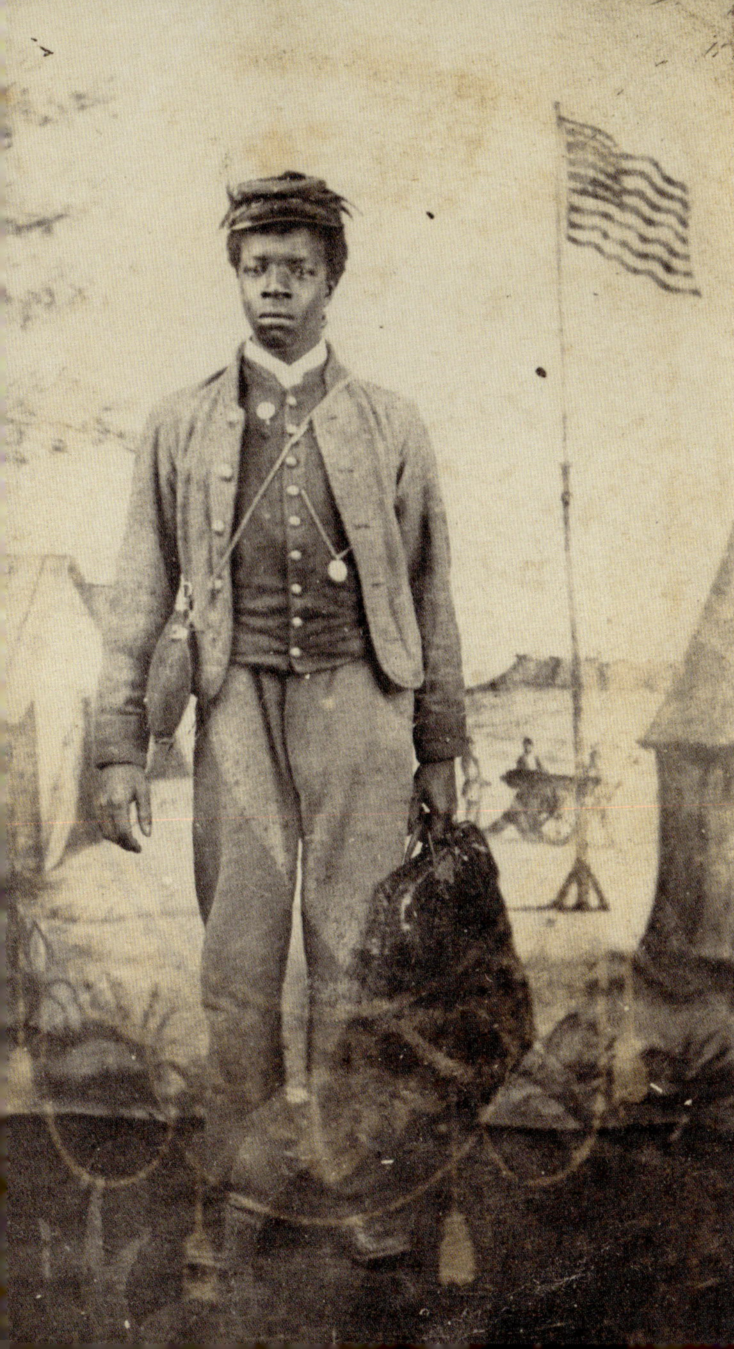

A young man wearing a military cap and carrying a canteen and valise, 1861–65
Unidentified photographer

A Negro History Week display created by Frances Albrier at the Emporium, San Francisco, California, 1957
Strohmeyer
Photographs

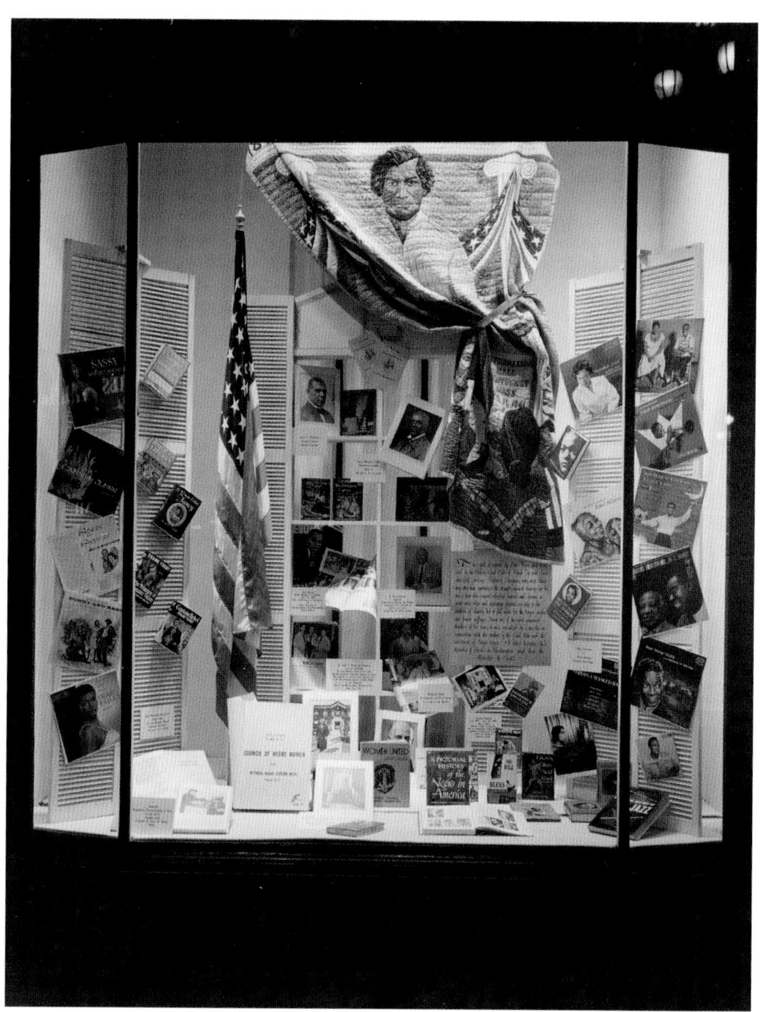

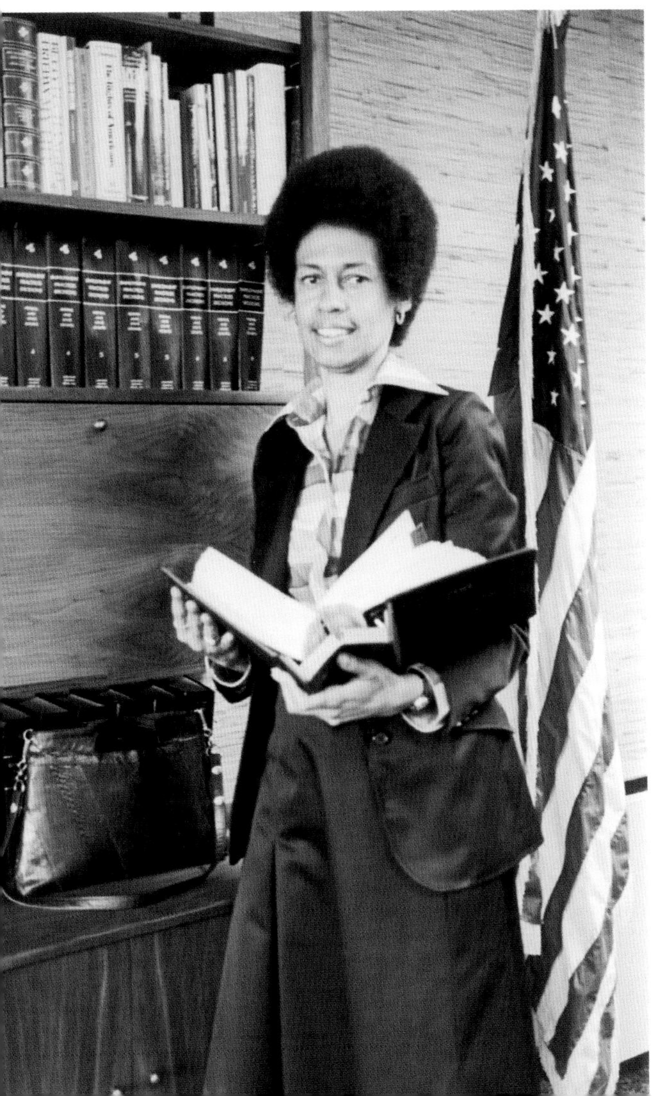

Eleanor Holmes Norton, chairwoman of the Equal Employment Opportunity Commission, holds a volume of employment practices decisions, 1977
Maurice Sorrell

—

Eleanor Holmes Norton was already a leader in the Feminist and Civil Rights Movements and chair of the New York City Commission on Civil Rights when President Jimmy Carter appointed her as the first woman to chair the U.S. Equal Employment Opportunity Commission (EEOC, 1977–81). At the EEOC, she settled tens of thousands of complaints and advocated for parallel actions to secure equal rights for minorities and women. After serving in the EEOC, she taught law, and in 1991 she ran for election to the U.S. House of Representatives as the non-voting delegate for the District of Columbia. A passionate proponent of full voting rights and statehood for D.C. residents, Norton was elected to her eighteenth term in 2024.

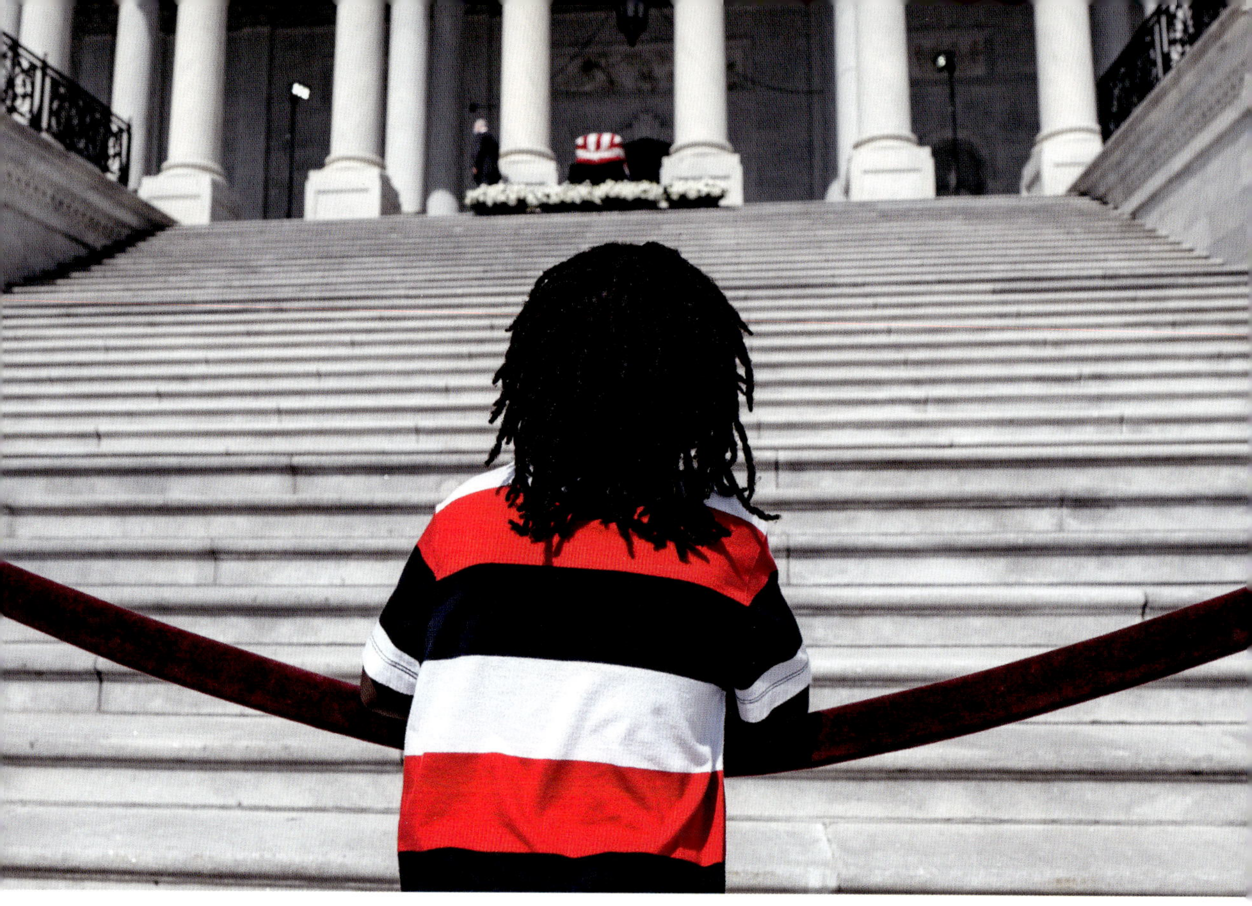

Jeremiah Harrell looks up at the casket of Rep. John Lewis as he lies in state on the steps of the U.S. Capitol, Washington, D.C., July 28, 2020
Michael A. McCoy

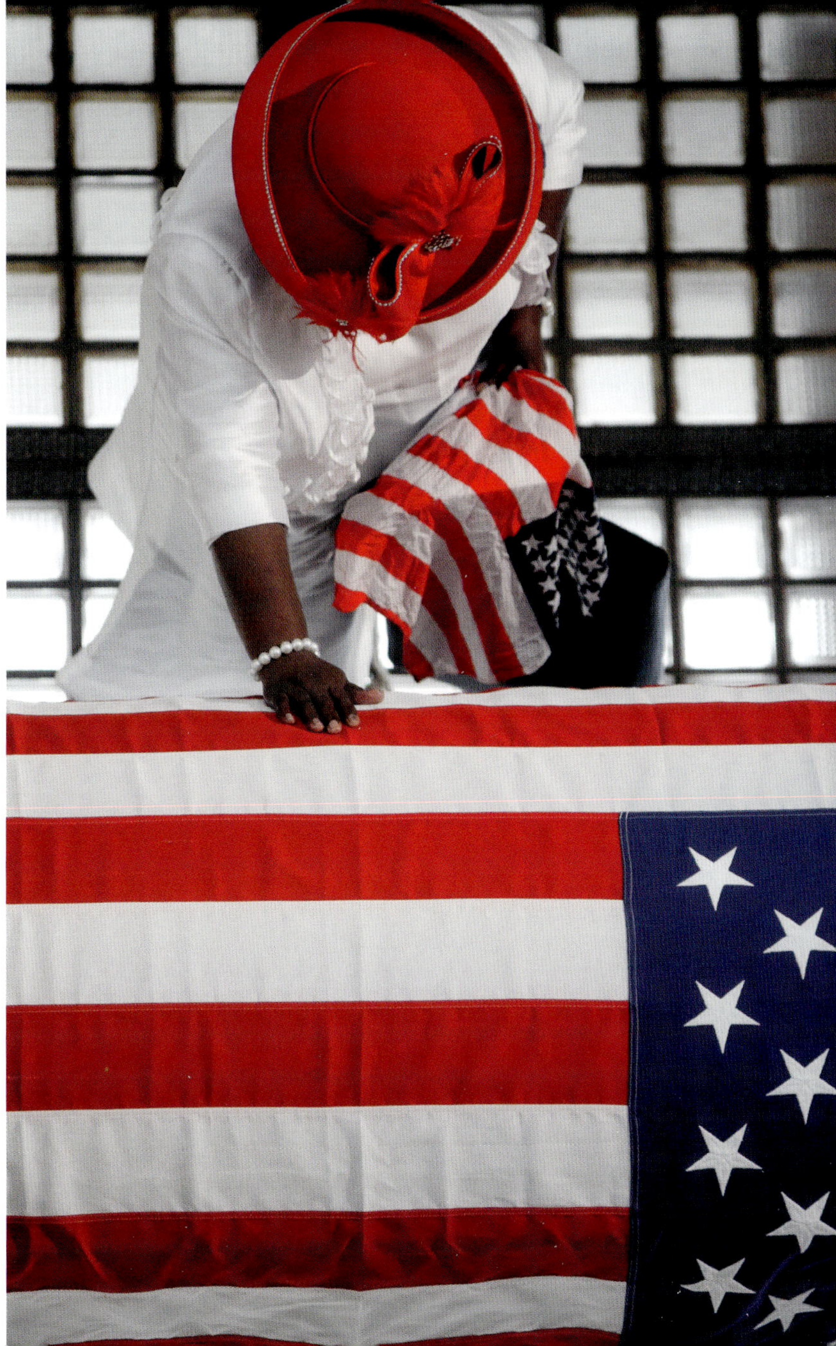

John Lewis
Memorials, Georgia 2
July 30, 2020
Chris Aluka Berry
—
Gussie Breedlove rests her
hand on Rep. John Lewis's
casket in the rotunda of
the Georgia State Capitol.

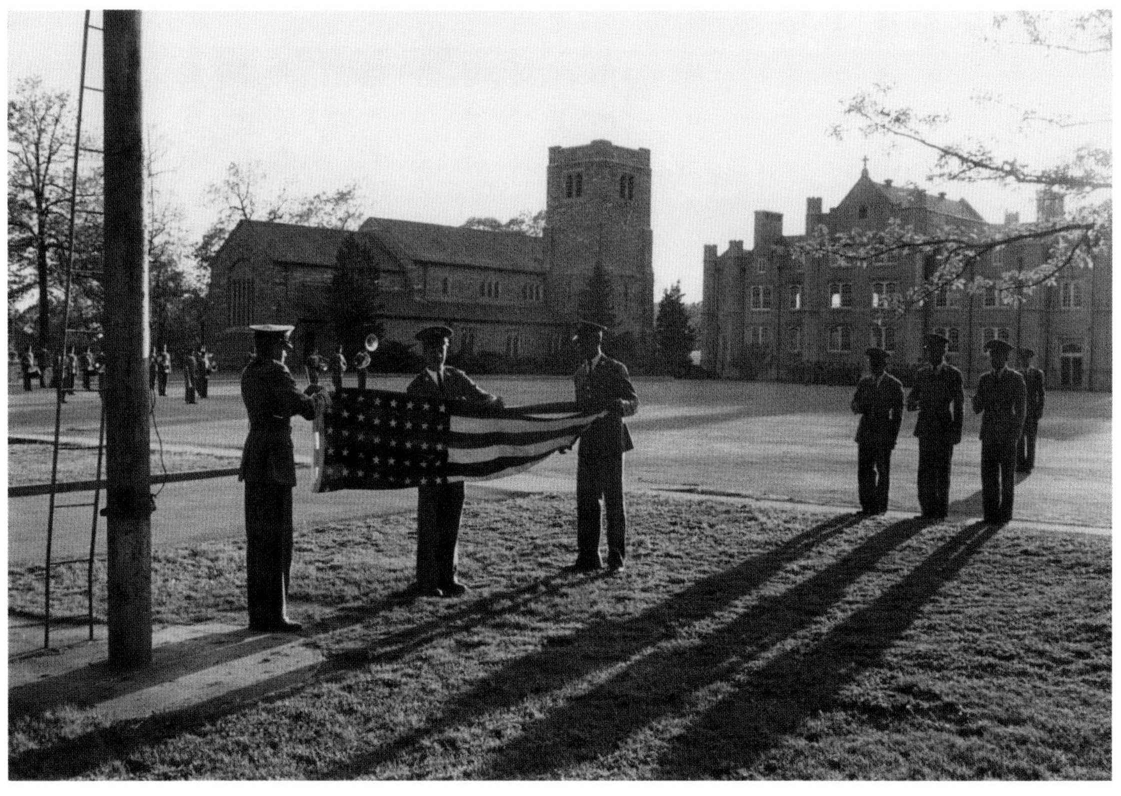

**Cadets at St. Emma
Military Academy,
Powhatan, Virginia,**
ca. 1955
Mike Shea

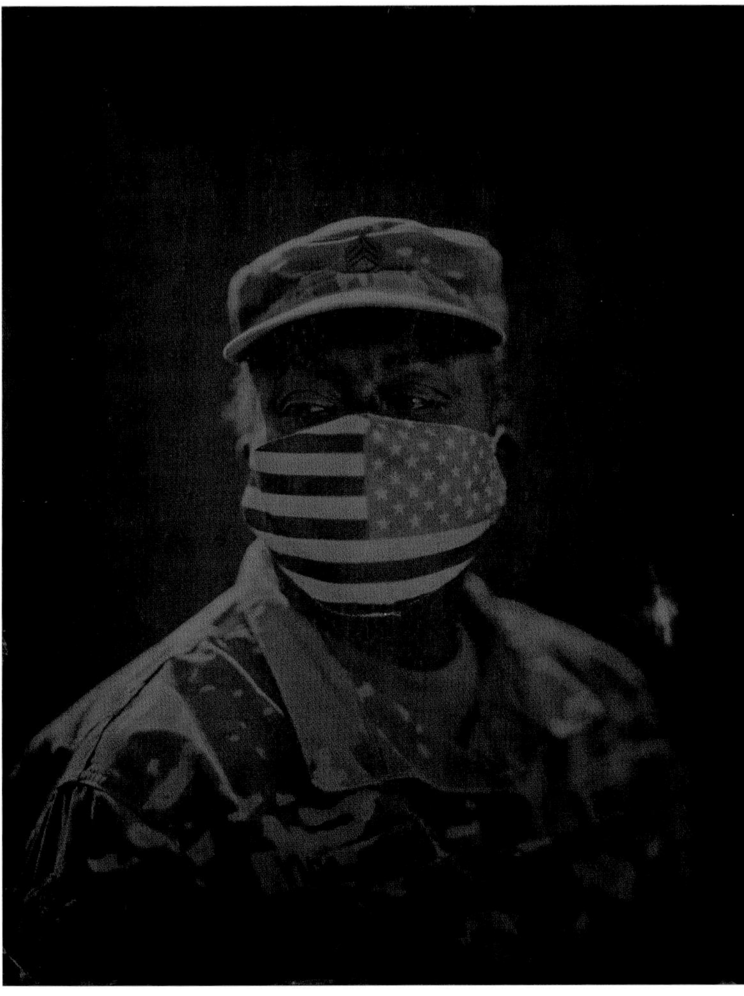

Soldier #2, 2020
From the series
My America
Rashod Taylor

**Campers salute
the American Flag,
Camp Atwater,
Massachusetts**,
ca. 1956
Bertrand Miles
—

Camp Atwater, the
oldest Black-owned and
-operated summer camp
in the United States,
was established in 1921
to provide recreational
opportunities for African
American children at a
time when most summer
camps were racially
segregated. The camp
boasts over 60,000
alumni, including costume
designer Ruth E. Carter
and Coleman A. Young,
former mayor of Detroit.

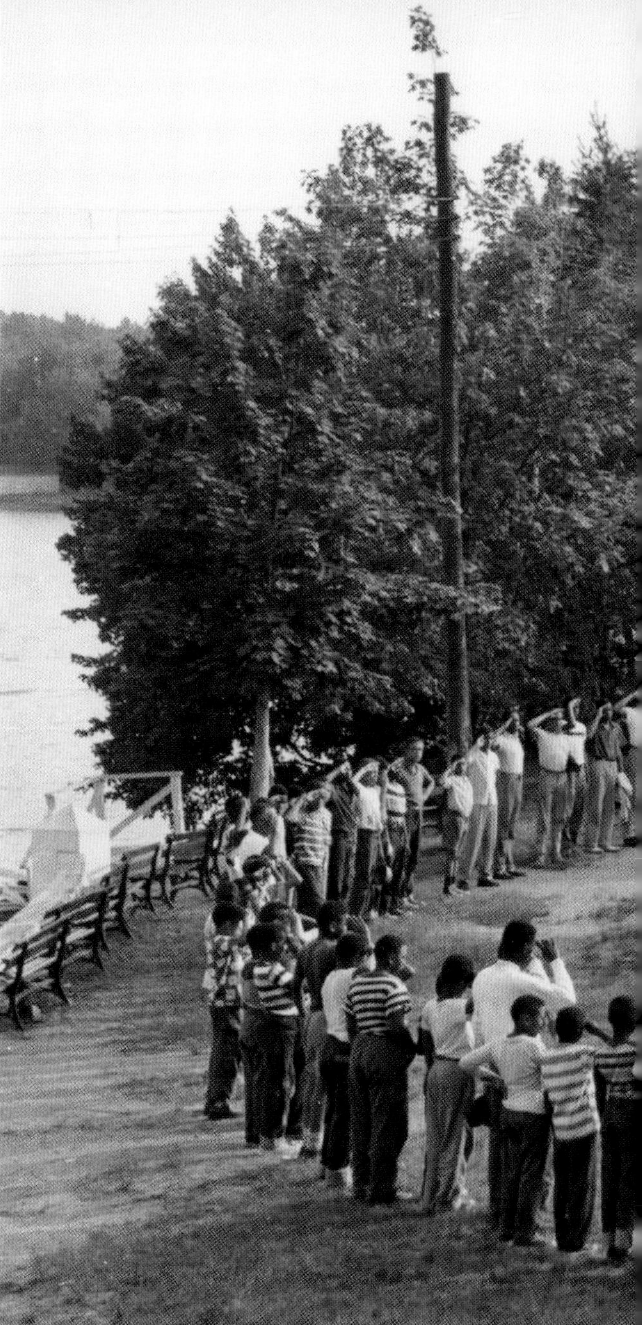

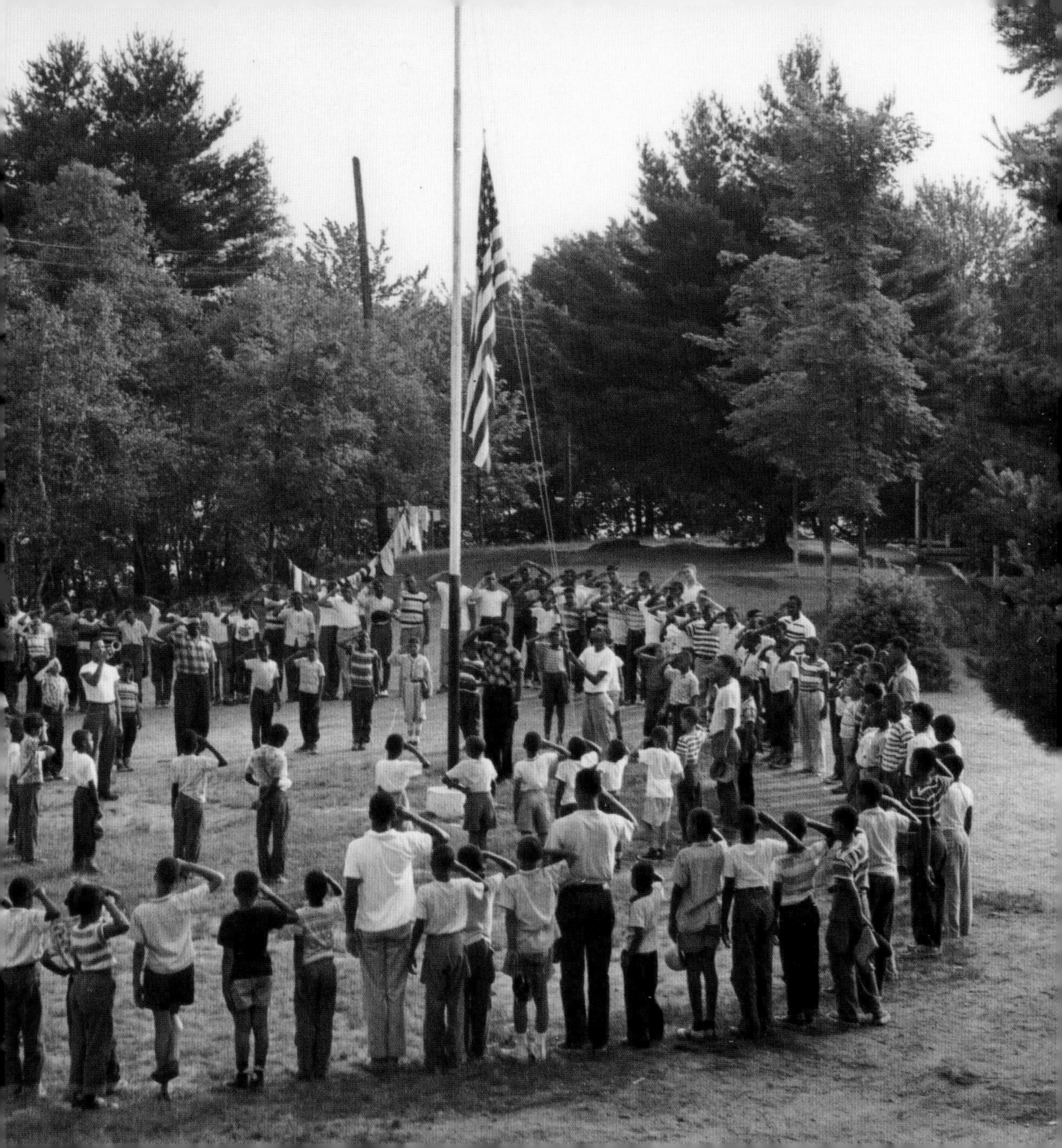

Sgt. William H. Carney with the U.S. flag carried by the 54th Massachusetts Infantry, ca. 1864
John Ritchie

—

Sergeant William Carney was awarded the Medal of Honor for his gallantry during actions at Battery Wagner on July 18, 1863, during the Civil War. When his unit's color guard was killed during the battle, Sergeant Carney—despite his own serious wounds—scrambled to retrieve the U.S. flag before it fell to the ground and carried it forward to the base of the fort, urging his fellow soldiers to follow him.

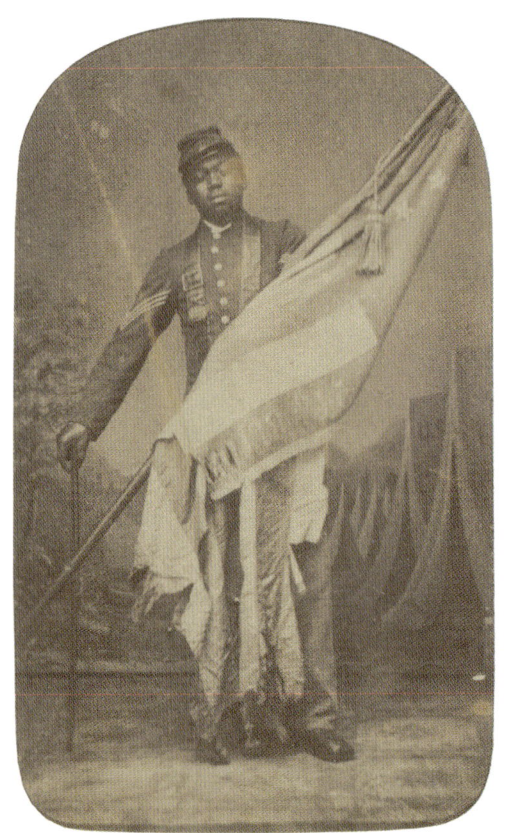

"Boys, I only did my duty; the old flag never touched the ground."

　　Sgt. William H. Carney

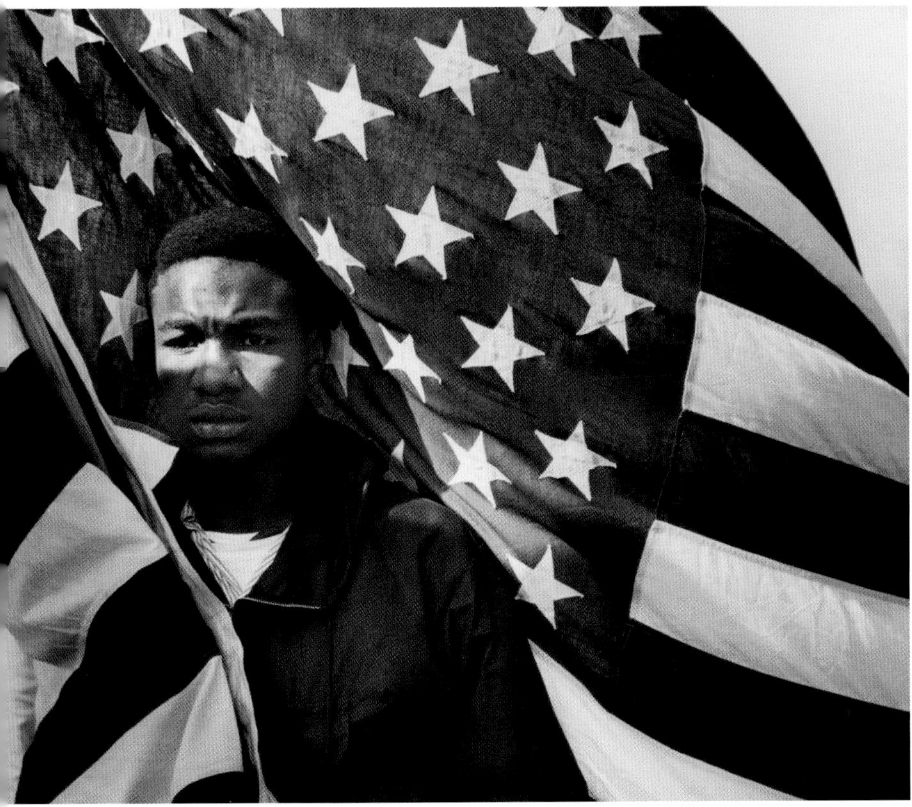

Lewis "Big June" Marshall Carrying the U.S. Flag, Selma to Montgomery March, March 21, 1965
James H. Karales

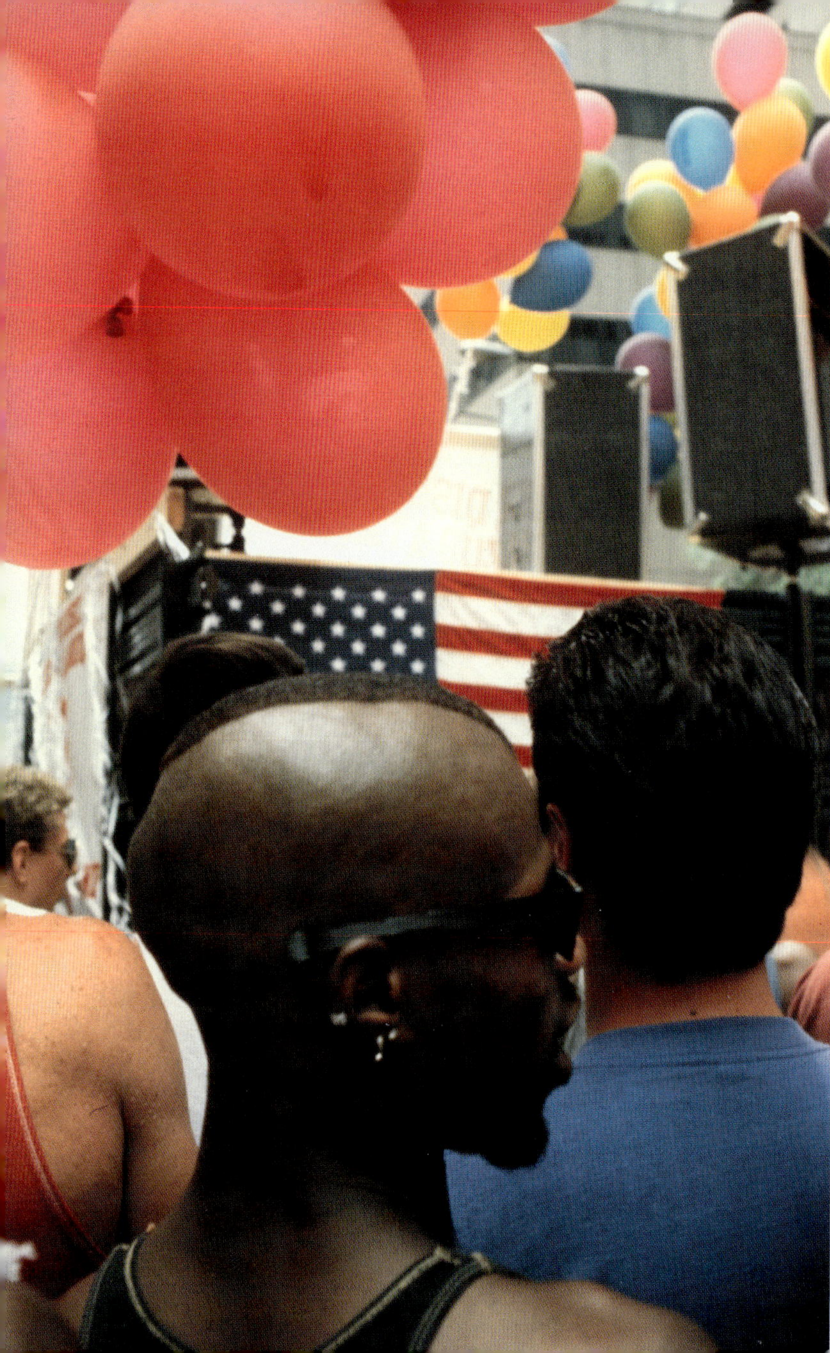

Participants at a New York Gay Pride Parade, 1980s
Ron Simmons

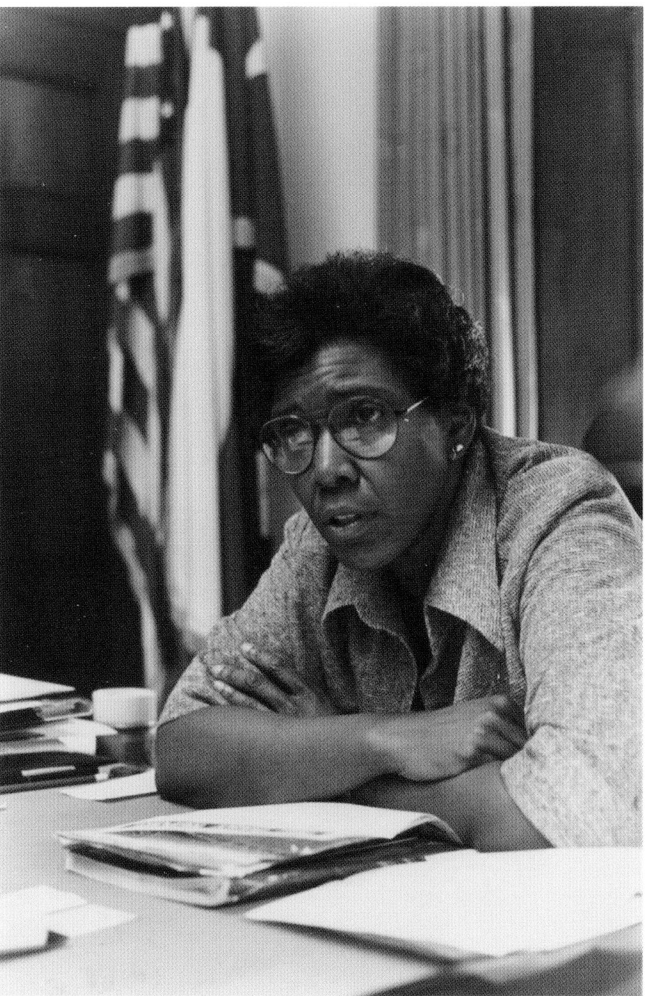

Barbara Jordan, 1970s
Maurice Sorrell

—

Barbara Jordan served in the Texas Senate from 1966 to 1972 and was the first Black woman elected to Congress from the South, serving in the U.S. House of Representatives from 1973 to 1979. Jordan was an outspoken and pragmatic champion for social justice, often building coalitions, seeking out powerful committee assignments, and working the system to get things done. In 1974, for the televised Judiciary Committee hearings considering articles of impeachment against President Richard M. Nixon, she delivered opening remarks in support of impeachment, stating "My faith in the Constitution is whole, it is complete, it is total. I am not going to sit here and be an idle spectator to the diminution, the subversion, and destruction of the Constitution."

Muhammad Ali, 2009;
printed 2019
Platon

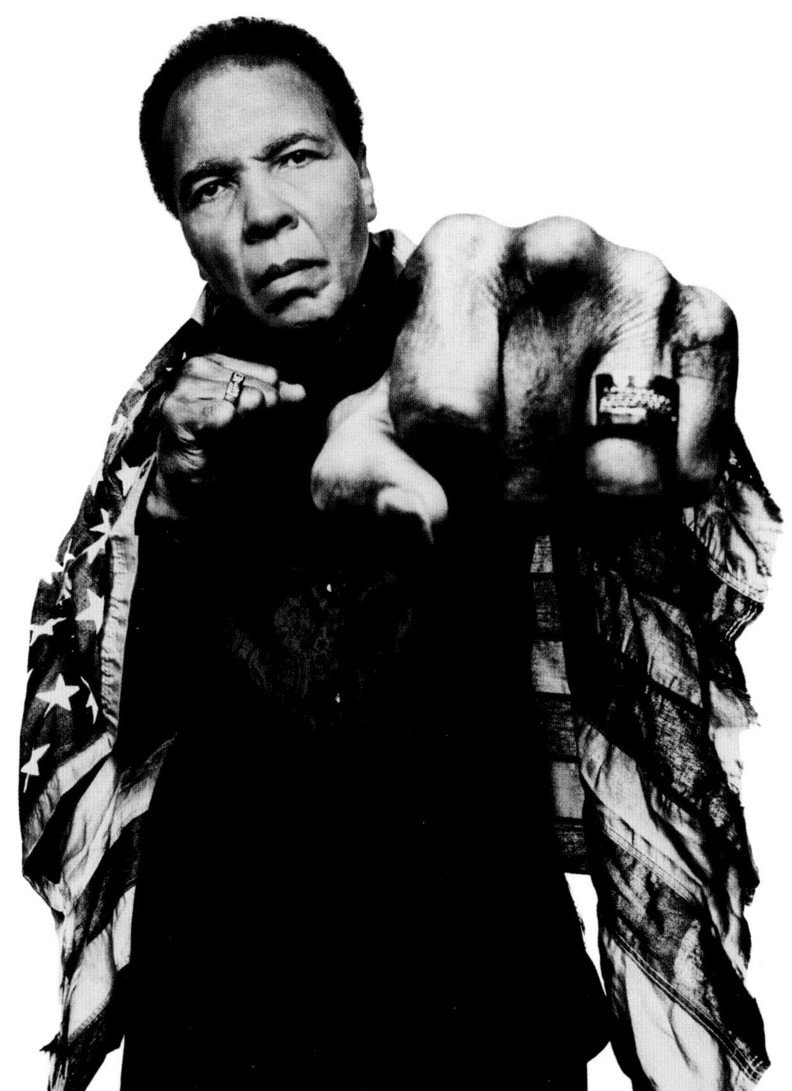

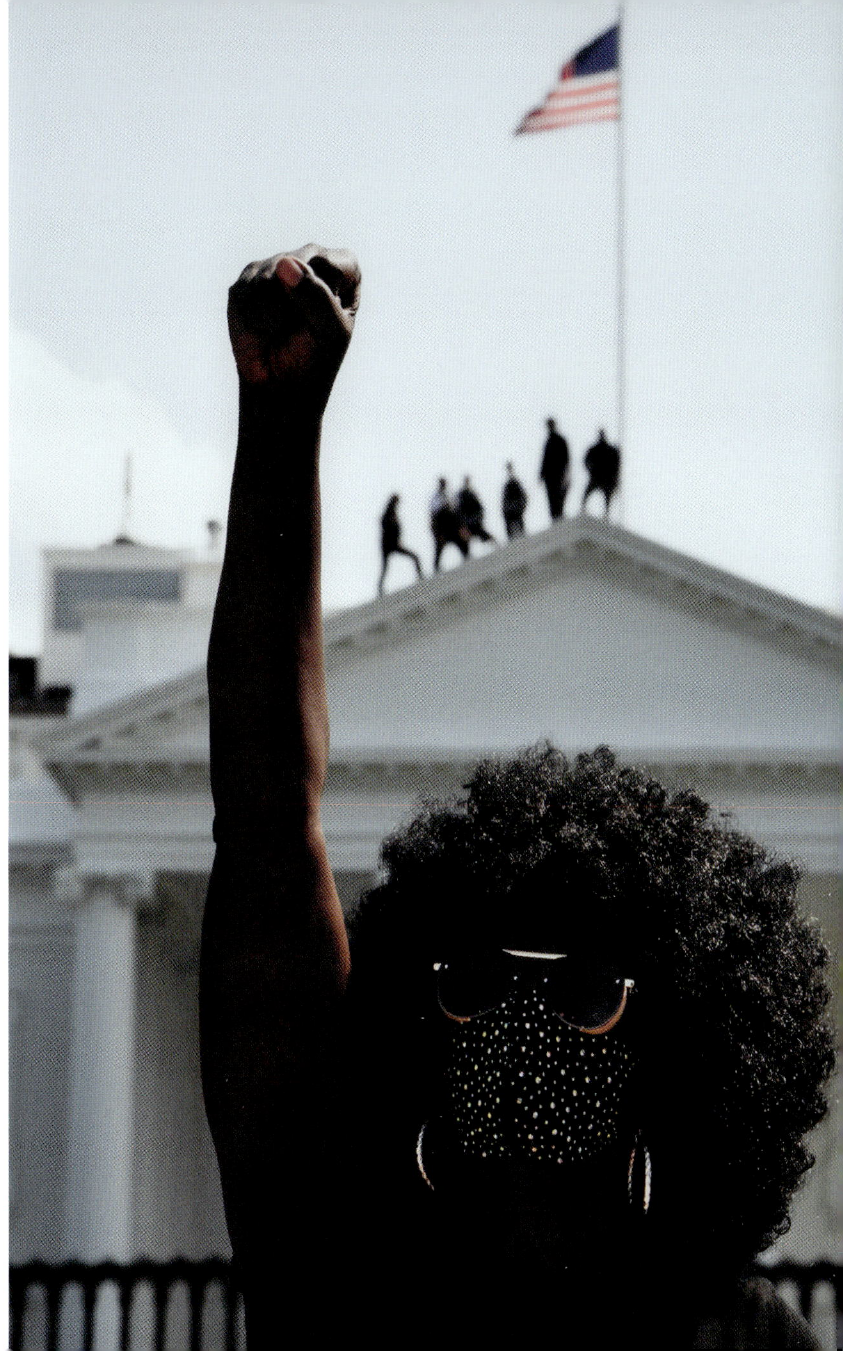

Pamela Weems in front of the White House, Washington, D.C., August 26, 2020; printed 2021
Matt McClain

Index

Unless otherwise noted, all photographic materials are in the collection of the National Museum of African American History and Culture. Photographs credited "Johnson Publishing Company Archive" are jointly owned by the National Museum of African American History and Culture and J. Paul Getty Trust. Made possible by the Ford Foundation, J. Paul Getty Trust, John D. and Catherine T. MacArthur Foundation, Andrew W. Mellon Foundation, and Smithsonian Institution.

Rev. Henry Clay Anderson
Members of the Improved Benevolent Protective Order of Elks of the World during a parade in Greenville, Mississippi,
mid-20th century
gelatin silver print
5 × 7 in. (12.7 × 17.8 cm)
Gift of Charles Schwartz and Shawn Wilson
2012.137.28.21
© Smithsonian National Museum of African American History and Culture
Page 29

Anthony Barboza
Jacksonville, Fla., 1968
gelatin silver print
9¾ × 6⅝ in. (24.8 × 16.8 cm)
2016.99.9
© Anthony Barboza
Page 21

Janette Beckman
Luther Campbell and the 2 Live Crew, 1990
inkjet print
9⅝ × 12 in. (24.5 × 30.5 cm)
2015.132.64.2
© Janette Beckman
Page 23

Chris Aluka Berry
John Lewis Memorials, Georgia 2,
July 30, 2020
digital image
Gift of Chris Aluka Berry
2024.72.6
© Chris Aluka Berry
Page 69

James P. Blair
The March on Washington,
August 28, 1963; printed ca. 2021
inkjet print
15 × 10 in. (38.1 × 25.4 cm)
Gift of Jim and Elise Blair
2021.67.6
© Estate of James P. Blair
Page 56

Sheila Pree Bright
Charles Cauthen, Age 19, African American, 2008; printed 2024
From the series *Young Americans*
archival pigment print
21⅝ × 16 in. (55 × 40.6 cm)
2024.68.2
© Sheila Pree Bright
Page 52

Sheila Pree Bright
Shanae Rowland, Age 21, American, 2008; printed 2024
From the series *Young Americans*
archival pigment print
21⅝ × 16 in. (55 × 40.7 cm)
2024.68.3
© Sheila Pree Bright
Page 50

Sheila Pree Bright
Wheatpasted photograph of Shanae Rowland on the side of a stairwell, Coconut Grove Neighborhood, Miami, Florida,
2008
digital image
Collection of Sheila Pree Bright
Courtesy of Sheila Pree Bright,
© Sheila Pree Bright
Page 51

Vandell Cobb
Patti LaBelle performing during the pregame show of Super Bowl XXXVI, February 3, 2002
digital image
Johnson Publishing Company Archive
Page 22

Gaston DeVigne
Helen Jackson, Supreme Court seamstress, 1957
digital image
Johnson Publishing Company Archive
© Estate of Gaston DeVigne
Page 30

Frank Espada
El Ministro, 1964; printed later
From the series *The Puerto Rican Diaspora Documentary Project*
inkjet print
24 × 36 in. (61 × 91.4 cm)
Purchased with funds provided by the Smithsonian Latino Initiatives Pool, administered by the Smithsonian Latino Center
2021.53.16
© Estate of Frank Espada
Page 43

Lola Flash
Back at You, 2020
From the series *syzygy, the vision*
archival pigment print
22½ × 33¾ in. (57.2 × 85.8 cm)
Purchased through the American Women's History Initiative Acquisitions Pool administered by the Smithsonian American Women's History Initiative
2021.57.5
© Lola Flash
Pages 33, 82 (detail)

Stanley Forman
The Soiling of Old Glory,
April 5, 1976
gelatin silver print
11 × 14 in. (27.9 × 35.6 cm)
Gift of Elmer J. Whiting III
2011.17.196
© 1976 Stanley Forman
Pages 13, 61

Leonard Freed
Harlem, New York • USA, 1963
gelatin silver print
10⅞ × 7⅛ in. (27.6 × 18.1 cm)
Gift of Brigitte Freed in memory of Leonard Freed
2009.36.7
© Leonard Freed/Magnum Photos
Page 48

Leonard Freed
A participant during the March on Washington, August 28, 1963; printed 2013
gelatin silver print
12¹⁵⁄₁₆ × 8¹¹⁄₁₆ in. (32.9 × 22 cm)
Gift of Brigitte Freed in memory of Leonard Freed
2016.123.1.17
© Leonard Freed/Magnum Photos
Page 57

James H. Karales
Flag-Bearing Marchers, Selma to Montgomery March, 1965
digital image
Gift of Monica Karales and the Estate of James Karales
2015.129.80
© Estate of James Karales, Courtesy of Howard Greenberg Gallery, New York
Page 55

James H. Karales
Lewis "Big June" Marshall Carrying the U.S. Flag, Selma to Montgomery March,
March 21, 1965
digital image
Gift of Monica Karales and the Estate of James Karales
2015.129.76
© Estate of James Karales, Courtesy of Howard Greenberg Gallery, New York
Page 75

Charles E. Kerfoot
Josephine Sampson, 1910s
gelatin silver print on cardboard
5 × 9¹⁄₁₆ in. (12.7 × 23 cm)
Gift of James M. Baxter
2021.13.12
Page 38

Zun Lee
Protestors in Ferguson, Missouri,
October 11, 2014
From the series *Black Love Matters*
digital image
Gift of Zun Lee
2016.52.15
© Zun Lee
Page 62

Raymond K. Martin
The Hall Johnson Choir,
ca. 1935–52
gelatin silver print
8⅛ × 10 in. (20.6 × 25.4 cm)
Gift of Dr. Eugene Thamon Simpson, Representative, Hall Johnson Estate
TA2013.166.1.2
Page 42

Matt McClain
Pamela Weems in front of the White House, Washington, D.C.,
August 26, 2020; printed 2021
archival pigment print
16¼ × 11 in. (41.3 × 27.9 cm)
2023.6
© The Washington Post
Page 79

Michael A. McCoy
Angela Holder holding a folded flag at a ceremony honoring her great uncle Cpl. Jesse Moore,
2024
digital image
Gift of Michael A. McCoy
2024.86.3
© Michael A. McCoy
Page 41

Michael A. McCoy
A cowgirl carrying an American flag at a rodeo, 2014
digital image
Gift of Michael A. McCoy
2024.86.5
© Michael A. McCoy
Frontispiece (detail), page 18

Michael A. McCoy
Father with child at Baltimore's AFRAM Festival, 2017
digital image
Gift of Michael A. McCoy
2024.86.9
© Michael A. McCoy
Page 46

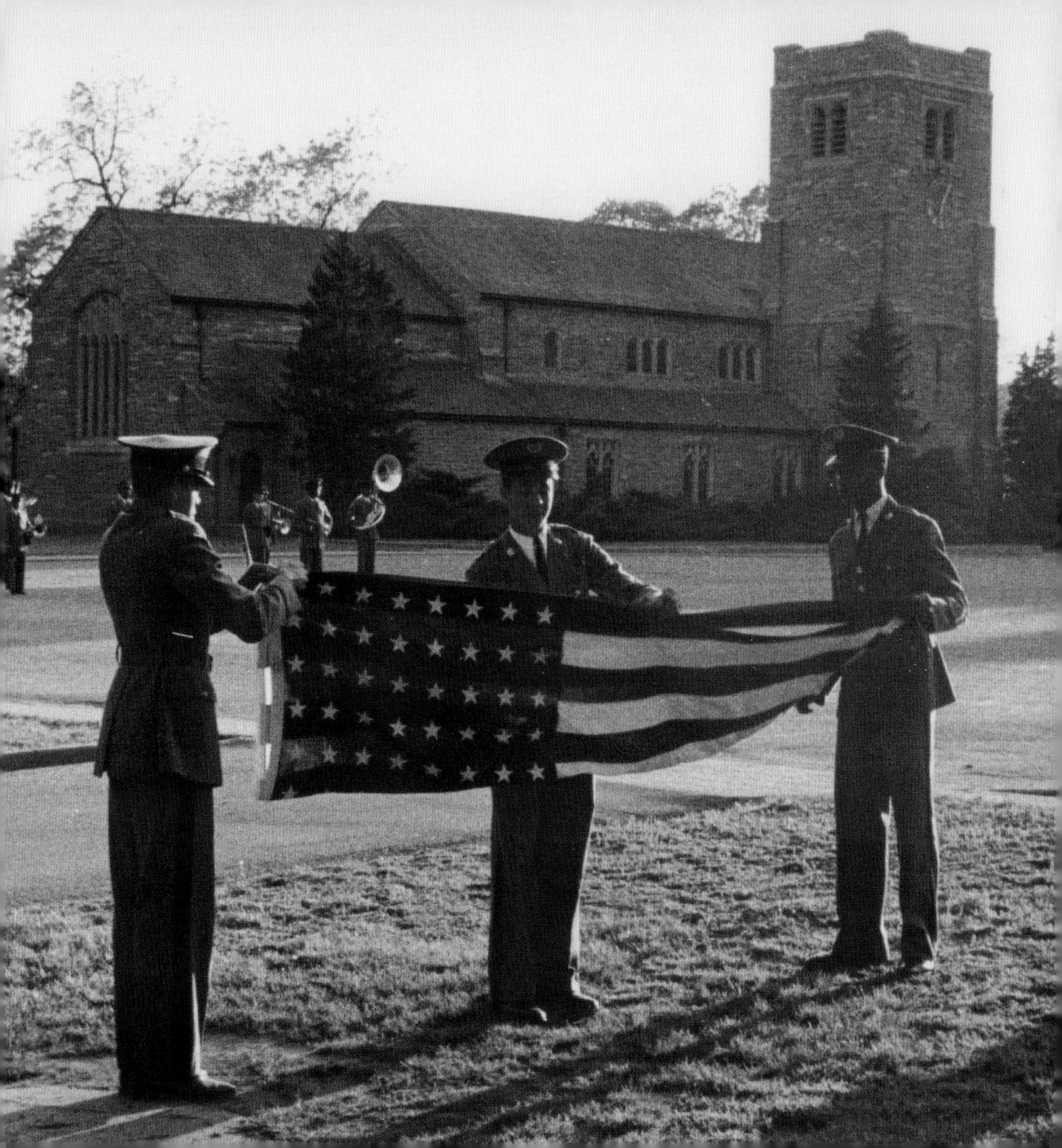

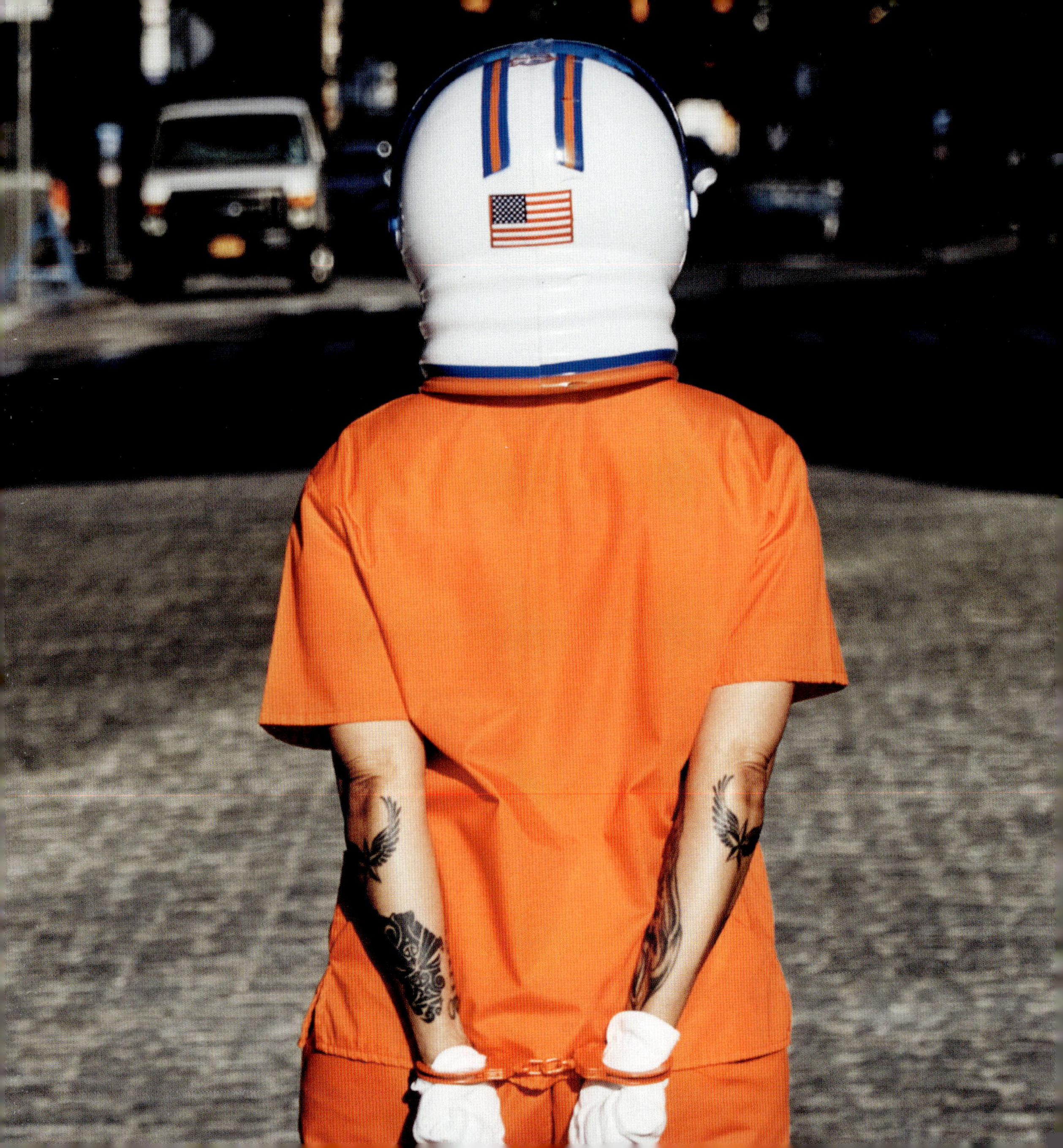

Michael A. McCoy
Jeremiah Harrell looks up at the casket of Rep. John Lewis as he lies in state on the steps of the U.S. Capitol, Washington, D.C., July 28, 2020
digital image
Gift of Michael A. McCoy
2024.86.6
© Michael A. McCoy
Page 68

Michael A. McCoy
Maj. Fannie Griffin McClendon (Ret.), 2022
digital image
Gift of Michael A. McCoy
2024.86.4
© Michael A. McCoy
Page 34

Michael A. McCoy
Vietnam veteran, Martinsburg, West Virginia, 2017
digital image
Gift of Michael A. McCoy
2024.86.8
© Michael A. McCoy
Page 27

Bertrand Miles
Campers salute the American Flag, Camp Atwater, Massachusetts, ca. 1956
digital image
Johnson Publishing Company Archive
Page 72

Bertrand Miles
Will Holland guarding George Washington's tomb, 1955
digital image
Johnson Publishing Company Archive
Page 31

James L. Mitchell
James Brown and Bootsy Collins perform during Brown's "Living in America" television concert, Los Angeles, California, June 1991
digital image
Johnson Publishing Company Archive
Page 53

Gordon Parks
American Gothic, 1942; printed later
gelatin silver print
14 × 11 in. (35.6 × 27.9 cm)
2024.73
Pages 6 (detail), 26

Platon
Muhammad Ali, 2009; printed 2019
archival pigment print
20¹⁵⁄₁₆ × 20 in. (53.2 × 50.8 cm)
Gift of Platon
2021.33.61
© Platon
Page 78

John Ritchie
Sgt. William H. Carney with the U.S. flag carried by the 54th Massachusetts Infantry, ca. 1864
albumen carte-de-visite
6¼ × 5 in. (15.9 × 12.7 cm)
Gift of the Garrison Family in memory of George Thompson Garrison
2014.115.8
Page 74

Mike Shea
Cadets at St. Emma Military Academy, Powhatan, Virginia, ca. 1955
digital image
Johnson Publishing Company Archive
Page 70

Ron Simmons
Participants at a New York Gay Pride Parade, 1980s
color slide
2 × 2 in. (5.1 × 5.1 cm)
Gift of Ron Simmons
TA2019.38.1.1.1.12
© Ron Simmons
Page 76

Moneta Sleet Jr.
Louis Armstrong's 70th birthday celebration at the Shrine Auditorium, Los Angeles, California, July 1970
digital image
Johnson Publishing Company Archive
Page 52

Maurice Sorrell
Barbara Jordan, 1970s
digital image
Johnson Publishing Company Archive
Page 77

Maurice Sorrell
Congresswoman Shirley Chisholm speaks at the Mary McLeod Bethune Statue Commemoration Celebration, Lincoln Park, Washington, D.C., 1971
digital image
Johnson Publishing Company Archive
Pages 17 (detail), 20

Maurice Sorrell
Eleanor Holmes Norton, chairwoman of the Equal Employment Opportunity Commission, holds a volume of employment practices decisions, 1977
digital image
Johnson Publishing Company Archive
Page 67

Maurice Sorrell
Fannie Lou Hamer and Ella Baker at the Mississippi Freedom Democratic Party Convention, Jackson, Mississippi, August 1964
digital image
Johnson Publishing Company Archive
Pages 11, 59

Strohmeyer & Wyman
Girls of the Booker Washington School, Tuskegee, Ala.—Mrs. McKinley in Near Carriage, 1899
albumen stereograph
3½ × 7 in. (8.9 × 17.8 cm)
2011.155.185
Page 44

Strohmeyer Photographs
A Negro History Week display created by Frances Albrier at the Emporium, San Francisco, California, 1957
gelatin silver print
9¾ × 8 in. (24.8 × 20.3 cm)
Frances Albrier Collection
2010.60.6
Page 66

Rashod Taylor
LJ and His Fort, 2020
From the series *Little Black Boy*
gelatin silver print
20 × 24 in. (50.8 × 61 cm)
2024.77.1
© Rashod Taylor
Page 47

Rashod Taylor
The Past, 2019
From the series *My America*
tintype
10 × 8 in. (25.4 × 20.3 cm)
2024.77.2
© Rashod Taylor
Page 36

Rashod Taylor
The Present, 2018
From the series *My America*
tintype
10 × 8 in. (25.4 × 20.3 cm)
2024.77.3
© Rashod Taylor
Page 37

Rashod Taylor
Soldier #2, 2020
From the series *My America*
tintype
10 × 8 in. (25.4 × 20.3 cm)
2024.77.5
© Rashod Taylor
Page 71

Roderick Terry
Flag Around Neck, October 16, 1995
From the series *One Million Strong*
gelatin silver print
13¹¹⁄₁₆ × 10⅝ in. (34.8 × 27 cm)
Gift of Roderick Terry
2013.99.49
© Roderick Terry
Page 25

Roderick Terry
Glory, October 16, 1995
From the series *One Million Strong*
gelatin silver print
13¹¹⁄₁₆ × 10⅝ in. (34.8 × 27 cm)
Gift of Roderick Terry
2013.99.54
© Roderick Terry
Page 64

Unidentified photographer
Carl Lewis after winning his fourth gold medal at the Los Angeles Olympics, 1984
chromogenic print
10 × 8 in. (25.4 × 20.3 cm)
Gift of Carl Lewis Estate
2012.154.32
Pages 15, 24

Unidentified photographer
Gen. Colin Powell's swearing in as chairman of the Joint Chiefs of Staff, 1989; inscribed later
chromogenic print
7½ × 9⁷⁄₁₆ in. (19 × 24 cm)
Gift of Alma J. Powell
A2022.101.1.8ab
Page 35

Unidentified photographer
A young man wearing a military cap and carrying a canteen and valise, 1861–65
albumen carte-de-visite
4 × 2⅜ in. (10.2 × 6 cm)
Gift from the Liljenquist Family Collection
2016.166.21
Page 65

James H. Wallace Jr.
Activist Leader Hillard Caldwell with American Flag, Facing a Policeman During a Demonstration, 1964
digital image
Gift of James H. Wallace Jr.
2011.11.4
Courtesy Jim Wallace Collection, Wilson Special Collections Library, UNC-Chapel Hill
Page 28

James H. Wallace Jr.
July 4 March through Chapel Hill, 1964
digital image
Gift of James H. Wallace Jr.
2011.11.6
Courtesy Jim Wallace Collection, Wilson Special Collections Library, UNC-Chapel Hill
Page 9

Frederick Watkins Jr.
Congressman Charles Rangel in his office, 1998
digital image
Johnson Publishing Company Archive
Page 49

Milton Williams
United States Air Force Honor Guard Pallbearers Carry the Flag-Draped Coffin of U.S. Air Force Four Star General Daniel "Chappie" James from an Air Force C-141 Starlifter Airplane at Andrews Air Force Base, Suitland, Maryland, February 26, 1978
gelatin silver print
10 × 8 in. (25.4 × 20.3 cm)
Gift of Milton Williams Archives
2011.15.237
© Milton Williams
Page 40